Dominica:

Isle of Adventure

Lennox Honychurch

M
CARIBBEAN

To my sister, Sara

First published 1991
Reprinted 1991, 1992 (twice), 1993

Published by THE MACMILLAN PRESS LTD
London and Basingstoke
*Associated companies and representatives in Accra,
Auckland, Delhi, Dublin, Gaborone, Hamburg, Harare,
Hong Kong, Kuala Lumpur, Lagos, Manzini, Melbourne,
Mexico City, Nairobi, New York, Singapore, Tokyo.*

ISBN 0 – 333 – 53007 – 1

Printed in Hong Kong

A catalogue record for this book is available from the
British Library.

Acknowledgements

The author and publishers wish to acknowledge, with thanks, the following photographic
sources:
Dr Peter Evans, Carol Kane, Michael Bourne, Dive Dominica, James Henderson, NDC.
All unattributed photographs, including those on the cover, are by Lennox Honychurch.

The publishers have made every effort to trace the copyright holders, but if they have
inadvertently overlooked any, they will be pleased to make the necessary arrangements
at the first opportunity.

| Contents |

Geneva Valley, Grand Bay (JAMES HENDERSON)

Foreword

The publication of this guide has been undertaken in response to the tremendous wave of interest shown by an increasing number of visitors who want to know more about Dominica. It gives the reader a comprehensive background to the history and natural features of the island with details of the different types of tropical forest from the seashore to the mountain tops. There are chapters on plants, wildlife, festivals and folklore, agriculture, handicrafts and guided tours of our national parks, mountain trails and coastal areas. Notes on hotels, restaurants and tour agencies are also included. This is our first locally-produced guide and it is all credit to Lennox Honychurch for the dedication with which he has prepared the text and photography out of a great love for the island and its people.

It is therefore a pleasure to recommend this book and I hope that it will serve to stimulate a greater awareness and understanding of this special island.

Gerry Aird
Chairman
Division of Tourism
National Development Corporation

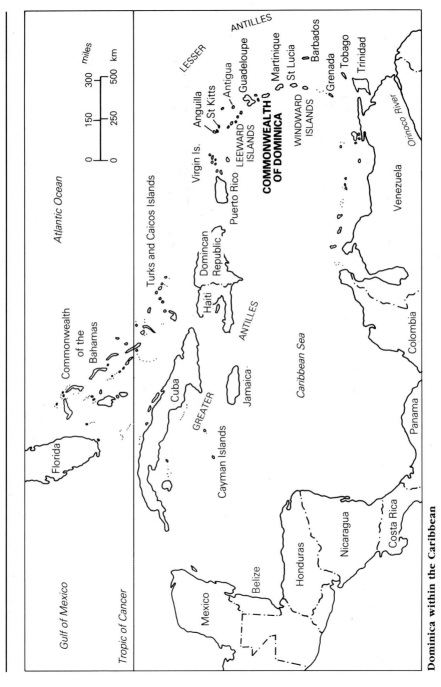

Dominica within the Caribbean

| 1 |

We are not the Dominican Republic

Dominica is an English-speaking island in the Windward Islands group of the Eastern Caribbean. But there is one Spanish sentence that every Dominican knows, and that is *Mal encaminado a Santo Domingo:* Missent to the Dominican Republic. It appears stamped in purple ink across many of the letters we receive from abroad. It is an inconvenience we have to live with. It always has to be emphasised that these are two completely different Caribbean states. The Dominican Republic is in the Greater Antilles, the Commonwealth of Dominica is in the Lesser Antilles.

The Columbus family has a lot to answer for where the people of Dominica are concerned. Christopher Columbus sighted the island on Sunday, 3 November, 1493 and christened it in Latin *Dominica* in honour of the Lord's Day. Five years later his brother Bartholomew established a city on the island of Hispaniola much further north

Bois Carib, *Sabinea carinalis,* **the national flower** (DR PETER EVANS)

1

and called it *Santo Domingo*. Over three centuries later the descendants of these settlers established *The Dominican Republic*, and since then the two islands have been tied in a knot of confused identity.

When the British colony of Dominica prepared for Independence in 1978, it considered the problem of nomenclature. Some suggested that the island should revert to its original Carib Indian name. But that was *Wai'tukubuli* and the majority considered it was too much of a mouthful. To make matters more confusing, Dominica was to become a republic, but the word 'republic' had to be avoided at all costs. So the government settled on the wording *Commonwealth of Dominica* which, as someone soon pointed out, has more letters in it than Wai'tukubuli!

Nevertheless, the confusion remains and every citizen of Dominica is resigned to the fact that whenever he goes abroad, or writes in the international press, he has to give a lesson in Caribbean geography. The simplest version goes:'The Dominican Republic is the big one next to Haiti, we are the small one further south.'

| 2 |
First impressions

Dominica has always been an adventurer's dream. The majestic luxuriance of its knotted terrain and forested slopes have captivated visitors for over five centuries. Scattered among ageing books and pamphlets one finds their fleeting references to the impact which the island has had upon them. Some encapsulate it in a sentence, viewed from the deck of a passing sailing-ship, others who have penetrated its valleys and secret cul-de-sacs ramble on for chapter after chapter. But always, however brief, there are the words 'green', 'blue', 'wild', 'beauty', and sometimes 'melancholy' brought on by the dominance of brooding mountains, roaring surf and tumbling streams.

Dominica is an island for travellers and adventurers rather than for those who like their pleasures manicured and tamed. As a visitor, one participates in the life of the island and enjoys its natural gifts of sea, river and mountain as the islanders do, whether on foot, by bus or car. In this way each new vista becomes a personal discovery rather than a programmed slot on a packaged itinerary. Here there is time to compare your impressions with those of the chroniclers who have been this way before.

The Caribs, paddling northwards up the chain of the Antilles one thousand years ago, came upon the rugged southern shoreline where steep cones rise sharply out of the raging sea and they christened this new island *Wai'tukubuli*: 'Tall is her body'. We have no record of the impressions of the Arawaks who had arrived another thousand years earlier, nor of the Ciboneys who were visitors even more distant in time.

From Nicolo Syllacio, an observant scribe on Christopher Columbus' second voyage to the Indies, we get the first written description of the island. Writing of the events which occurred on the 3 November, 1493, when Columbus first sighted Wai'tukubuli and renamed it Dominica, Syllacio notes that: *Dominica is remarkable for the beauty of its mountains and the amenity of its verdure and must be seen to be believed.*

That bland cliché at the end of his statement can be forgiven when

we remember that less than a hundred Europeans had ever seen the marvels of a tropical island before and that this was their first sight of the volcanic Caribees.

Most of the roving privateers, admirals and merchant captains who found shelter and refreshment on Dominica during the following two centuries commented on some aspect of the island's natural luxuriance. Sir Francis Drake, John Hawkins, Sir Richard Grenville and Christopher Newport were among them. Sir Anthony Sherley, calling in at Prince Rupert's Bay with nine storm-racked ships and their miserable crews in 1596, logged one of the earliest records of Dominican hospitality:

> *Arriving at Dominica the seventeenth of October, with all our men sicke and feeble, wee found there two hote bathes, wherein our weake men washing themselves were greatly comforted: and the Indians of this place used us with great kindnesse, so that we were all perfectly well before we departed from this place.*

Pere Labat, a friar of the Dominican Order, a ribald character and adventurous gourmet, paid us a visit in 1700. More interested in the Caribs and the tastiness of their cuisine than the nature of the island itself, his offhand comment on the landscape was that: *We walked right across the island to the windward coast seeing nothing more interesting than trees,* admitting later however that, *these trees were certainly the finest in the world.*

As colonisation intensified and visitors increased, the commentary becomes more varied but still always dominated by the foliage. Resident Attorney and Magistrate Thomas Atwood writing in 1791, produced the first promotional material for Dominica with tempting descriptions aimed at attracting the prospective settler rather than the casual tourist:

> *The taking of a morning or evening's walk in this island, by the sides of the rivers, whose glassy surface glides swiftly on, or murmuring waterfalls foam into view is very pleasing . . . Is he fond of the delightful study of botany; here an extensive field is open for his speculation, and numberless curious*

L'anse de Mai *(opposite)*

shrubs, plants and flowers, that grow spontaneously afford him ample scope for enquiry.

It was Atwood who came closest to figuring out the correct number of rivers in Dominica. Not the modern tourism promoter's 365, but more accurately:

There being upwards of thirty five rivers in the island, besides great numbers of rivulets of excellent fresh water.

The Victorian travellers in the following century, enthused with a spirit of imperial adventure, waxed even more poetic. The novelist and post office official Anthony Trollope stood on the deck of his visiting ship in 1856 and commented:

To my mind, Dominica as seen from the sea, is by far the most picturesque of all these islands. Indeed it would be difficult to beat it either in colour or grouping. It fills one with an ardent desire to be off and rambling among those green mountains.

The eccentric William Palgrave, who in 1876 had already seen much of the world, and was among the first visitors to make it to the Boiling Lake in the centre of the island, was even more ecstatic:

In the wild grandeur of its towering mountains, some of which rise to five thousand feet above the level of the sea; in the majesty of its almost impenetrable forests; in the gorgeousness of its vegetation, the abruptness of its precipices, the calm of its lakes, the violence of its torrents, the sublimity of its waterfalls, it stands without rival, not in the West Indies only, but I should think throughout the whole island catalogue of the Atlantic and Pacific combined.

The British historian James Anthony Froude came ten years later, not to observe nature, but to lament Britain's inability to come to grips with this wild island: *England has done nothing, absolutely nothing, to introduce her own civilization; and thus Dominica is English only in name.* But the island, as always, got the better even of this lofty imperialist, and soon he too was joining the chorus:

The mountains being the tallest in all the group, the rains are also the most violent and the ravines torn out by the torrents are the wildest and the most magnificent ... the sea if

possible, a deeper azure; the air more transparent; the forest
a lovelier green than I ever saw in any other country.

In the twentieth century we turn to the novelists and travel writers for a far deeper response to the impact of the island upon the senses. Alec Waugh, in three books, *Hot Countries, The Sugar Islands* and *The Fatal Gift*, loses his heart to Dominica. On his first visit in the 1920s he could not believe that anything could be so green:

I had never thought of green as being a colour that could
dazzle you. I had not believed that there could be so many
shades of green, that a single colour could have so many
varieties of tone and texture, could achieve such an effect of
patchwork.

Patrick Leigh Fermor in *The Traveller's Tree* captures the dual character of the island's coastline:

Windwardside is the region of daybreak and morning, and
of thousands of clouds blown up by the wind from the
turbulent waves. Leewardside is the country of the afternoon
and sunset, of the clear blue sky where the clouds have shed
their harm; of smooth reefs and lagoons and the glittering
waters of a sea walled in by a drowned mountain range . . .

In fiction, the power of the land itself becomes a dominant factor in the flow and plot of every novel set in Dominica. My grandmother Elma Napier, writing under the pen-name Elizabeth Garner, moulds her novel *Duet in Discord* around the story of an older woman sharing her passion for the island with a much younger lover; at one point reminding him that: *'like' is of all words the most ridiculous with which to express the love that I have for this place, love that has something almost physical about it so that in moments of pain I have quite literally lain full length and drawn solace from the ground . . . sometimes I know you must dream of the swirl of water on the point and remember the river running deep under the tree ferns.*

The novelist Jean Rhys was born in Dominica at the end of the last century, and although she departed the island when only sixteen years old, it left a mark upon her mind which lasted a lifetime and

Porte La Fin: The Gates of Hell, at Calibishie. A natural arch which once existed over the gateway collapsed in 1954 *(overleaf)*

was the thread which ran through all her work. In *Wide Sargasso Sea*, lovers, this time on their honeymoon, also become entwined with the forces of the island. Here the beauty of the land and the bride become one. A bewitching mixture, too intense for the bridegroom: *Everything is too much . . . too much blue, too much purple, too much green. The flowers too red, the mountains too high, the hills too near . . .*

Perhaps the people of the island take its scenery for granted, living every day surrounded by rivers, rainbows and colours of an ever-changing sky. In her novel *The Orchid House* Phyllis Allfrey noted this attitude through the eyes of the old family nursemaid who is the central character of her book:

> *I myself gazed outwards at the scene around me trying to see what there was in this common everyday outlook of mountains and blueness which filled my girls with passionate admiration. All I could see was a riot of gold and purple and crimson . . . and the two huge mango trees, the shining silver from against the damp wall and the purple shadows on far hills. Nothing unusual, except to those who had lived like exiles in grey shadows.*

For many however, the island never loses its fascination. Swimming through the cold, clear water of a river pool, sitting beneath the spray of a waterfall or watching a familiar mountain change colour in the afternoon light are the experiences of which I never tire. Always there seems to be another valley to explore, a peculiar rock formation or unusual orchid to investigate, and among the people, some charming twist of phrase, a new drop of wisdom from a local philosopher. 'How much farther is it to Grand Frond?' an acquaintance of mine once asked a wayside farmer. And waving his hand eastwards across the mountains in a helpful manner he replied, 'Oh just a little over and beyond.'

Even though it may at first appear to be a relatively small island, every corner cannot be covered, even in a lifetime. Some parts will always remain half-shrouded in mountain mist or seen at a distance through a swirl of sea spray. Such places must be left to one's own imagination or sense of adventure.

The shorter of the two Trafalgar Falls flows from the Breakfast River which is forded on the way to the Boiling Lake (*opposite*)

| 3 |
History

Dominica was first inhabited by Stone Age tribes from the Orinoco region of South America about 3000 BC. There were successive waves of these immigrants; among them shell fish gatherers, chippers of stone tools, nomadic hunters and fishermen drifting up the island chain in their roughly hewn dugouts. The earliest groups left little or nothing to record their passing, but those we call the Ciboney left their chipped and worked stone and conch shell gouges scattered along the headlands near the sea or along river estuaries.

At about the time of Christ, the first of the Arawak-speaking tribes took up residence here. More sophisticated than those before them and more artistic than the Caribs who were to supersede them, the Arawaks were agriculturalists, fishermen and hunters.

In the excavated middens and dwelling sites we have found wonderful representations of the natural life of Dominica. Parrots, agoutis, turtles, frogs and bats form the subjects of their decorative pottery. Designs in white, ochre and red embellish the clay pots and ceremonial incense burners. It all conjures up idyllic visions of man in harmony with the natural pulse of the island, free to roam the sea and up along the river valleys into the wonder of the undisturbed forest.

By 1000 AD the Caribs had entered the Lesser Antilles, pushing their way up the islands, dominating them one by one. Was the meeting of these tribes a clash of clubs and spears? A couple of years of massacre, blood and suppression? Or was it, as some archaeologists and historians now claim, a gradual infiltration and domination by the Caribs over the Arawaks, coupled with a decline of the classic period of Arawak culture on the islands?

Whatever happened, the Caribs were in complete control when seventeen shiploads of bearded, white-skinned men turned up off the east coast of Dominica on 3 November, 1493. The word 'discovery' in this context always irritates me. To say that Christopher Columbus 'discovered' Dominica in 1493 is rather like

Dominican National costume (CAROL KANE) *(opposite)*

saying that Julius Caesar 'discovered' Britain in 55 BC. I may be accused of semantics, but I always prefer to say that the island was 'sighted' by the adventurous Genoese navigator.

This was the first landfall of his second voyage to the Caribbean. To Columbus, this green mass was, like all the other islands, anonymous, and since it was early Sunday morning, he christened it in Latin *Dominica* in honour of the Lord's Day. Nice and simple in comparison to the florid prefixes he gave to the other island names further north, which he called after saints and Spanish monasteries.

Arriving off the treacherous eastern cliffs of Dominica, the little armada was unable to land and after skirting the north-east coast without success, the ships moved on to Marie Galante and Guadeloupe, which had also been sighted and named that morning.

One caravel was ordered to sail around the leeward side of Dominica in search of a protected anchorage, and found a splendid harbour at what is now Prince Rupert's Bay, where they reported seeing dwellings and people. Because of Dominica's position in the centre of the arc of the Lesser Antilles, it stands in the direct path of the sailing route from the Canary Islands, using the north-easterly Trade Winds. In the years ahead it became an important stop for refreshment of ships of all nations, and this bay at Portsmouth was the centre of most of the activity. It was a depot for outward-bound Spanish treasure trips and a haunt for the most famous pirates and privateers. Fresh water, hot springs, timber, firewood and trade with the Caribs for fresh fruit and cassava cakes made it a popular stop.

Because of the rugged terrain and Carib strength on the island, no colonisation occurred, and the people of Wai'tukubuli were able to hold on to their island for some 250 years after Columbus' arrival. During that period it was a base for Carib forces to launch attacks on the fledgling French and English colonies on the other islands.

When French settlers did eventually begin colonisation in the early eighteenth century, Dominica was, along with St Vincent, the last of the West Indies still under some form of Carib control. In spite of a neutrality agreement in 1686, renewed in 1748 under the Treaty of Aix-la-Chapelle, French settlement continued and expanded. Visiting lumbermen soon became farmers. Wood and grass thatched houses soon became stone and shingled ones. In retaliation for what they considered a breach of the neutrality treaty, the British attacked and captured the island in 1761. It was later ceded to Britain by the Treaty of Paris in 1763.

An idyllic setting for a cricket match at Atkinson

British colonisation was swift and throrough. All available land was surveyed into lots of not more than 300 acres each and then sold by public auction in Britain. Towns and fortifications were established, customs dues and regulations were set up, a House of Assembly was elected, and a printing press was imported. The importation of slaves from West Africa increased rapidly as plantations were opened up and Roseau and Portsmouth were declared free ports open to ships flying any flag at times of peace. Within a decade all the trappings of an eighteenth century plantocracy were firmly in place.

A large French population still held sway over agricultural production and commerce, while the British held the military and administrative power, thus creating a cultural mix which has endured for centuries.

The French regained the island for five years during the American War of Independence from 1778 to the end of 1783, but it was returned to Britain by the Treaty of Versailles, signed that same year. The confusion caused in the Caribbean by the French Revolution gave the French another chance in 1795, but their invasion force was scattered soon after landing. A last attempt to wrest the island from the British was made in 1805, when Napoleonic forces captured the

15

island for a few days, held the members of the Legislature hostage, and left with a ransom of £8,000, after demanding £12,000 to begin with.

The threat to British interests was internal as well as external. Maroon encampments formed by escaped slaves had spread among the forested hills in the centre of the island. An unofficial war of skirmishes, raids, ambushes, capture, torture and executions was waged among those hills from 1780 to 1814, as the British militia system clashed with the Maroons' guerilla tactics. One has but to glimpse Dominica from the air to appreciate how the complex formation of the central mountains aided the escaped slaves. The terrain of deep valleys and puzzling ridges was an excellent hideout. Hurricanes also took their toll on the colonists, and the isolation of estates made planters insecure and export of crops difficult.

Emancipation of the enslaved population came in 1834, with a brief 'apprenticeship' period ending in 1838. By then, coffee blight, another severe hurricane and falling sugar prices and production had forced Dominica into severe economic depression.

While the plantations struggled on, a new peasantry was beginning to emerge – the foundation of Dominica's modern farming community. The introduction of limes and cocoa processing improved the island's fortunes at the turn of the century. New roads were being built and bridges now spanned the larger streams. Telephones, electricity and motor cars were being introduced.

Yet another period of depression hit in the 1930s and 1940s, but Dominica found prosperity again in the 1950s, when bananas, the 'green gold', emerged as the main crop. Opening up and sale of Crown Lands in the interior gave a boost to agriculture and British and foreign aid funds provided services and infrastructure for the building of a new society.

Politically, Dominica's self-determination began in 1925, with a new constitution for elected representation. The founding of the first trade union and the expansion of local government through the formation of elected village councils led to increased awareness of the responsibilities of leadership. Gradually other constitutional changes took place, and Universal Adult Suffrage – the right for every citizen over the age of twenty-one to vote without property qualifications – was granted in 1951. Total self-government under the system of Associated Statehood with Britain was achieved in 1967, and the final ties of foreign affairs and defence were cut when

State House in Roseau (MICHAEL BOURNE)

Dominica became an independent republic – *The Commonwealth of Dominica* – in 1978 on 3 November. A date which, 465 years earlier, had changed the tall, green island of Wai'tukubuli for ever.

The form of government which was established by the new constitution of 1978 is headed by a President elected by the House of Assembly. There is a Cabinet of Ministers, headed by a Prime Minister, which is composed of members of the House of Assembly whose party holds the majority of seats in the House. General elections to fill the twenty-one elected seats in this Assembly are held every five years. Nine nominated Senators also sit in the same chamber. They are appointed by the President: five on the advice of the Prime Minister and four on the advice of the Leader of the Opposition. This makes up a unicameral legislature of thirty-one members including the Speaker of the House.

| 4 |
Agriculture

The national motto emblazoned on the coat of arms of the Commonwealth of Dominica declares in traditional French Creole patois: *Apres Bondie C'est La Ter*, After God it is the Land. Those few words symbolise what to most Dominicans is the essential natural pattern of their lives. In spite of a rise in business and public sector employment over the last two decades, every islander is ultimately reliant on the viability of agricultural production.

The lush climate and steep terrain of Dominica make it suitable for an agricultural system which is based largely on tree crops whose roots bind the soil. The land is so fertile and well-watered that one has but to stick a cutting in the ground and shoots appear in no time.

Some areas are known for the production of certain crops and vegetables. The highland villages around Roseau such as Giraudel, Bellevue Chopin, Morne Prosper, Trafalgar, Cochrane and Laudat are renowned for their vegetables. Pennville, Paix Bouche and Vieille Case are known for yams. Good Hope to Petite Savanne and Bagatelle are known for Bay Leaf production. The north east has the majority of coconuts. The Layou Valley has a concentration of citrus and bananas. The south around Soufriere now grows aloes. These are by no means hard and fast boundaries and a little of almost every tropical crop is spread liberally around the island.

The last thirty years have seen a marked change in the landholding pattern of Dominica. Large estates have been broken up, large tracts of Crown Lands in the interior sold off as part of Government land settlement schemes, agricultural land near towns and villages has been turned over to housing. This has put a severe strain on the land. Already ecological changes are being noticed in river flow and erosion patterns as small holdings are opened up along the mountain ridges. The extension of 'feeder roads' stretching like ever-growing fingers from the coastal villages into the forested hinterland follow land settlement. Agricultural chemicals now affect the lower reaches of some streams.

The average farm size in Dominica is about 10 acres although quite a large percentage are below that figure. Throughout our history, women have been important landholders. The tradition usually stems from mothers taking the intiative to save, negotiate and secure land for the maintenance of their families. There are also complex landholding arrangements known as 'family land' where relatively large tracts have been left in common for all the descendants of a particular ancestor. The Carib Territory, for instance, operates as one large piece of family land.

Coffee, cocoa, limes, vanilla beans, oranges and grapefruit have all had their turn at being Dominica's main export crop over the last two centuries. Today the biggest money-earner is bananas, shipped weekly to the United Kingdom by the British purchasing company, Geest Industries Ltd.

Since the 1960s coconut cultivation has risen rapidly. A local public company, Dominica Coconut Products processes the island's entire crop for export. Growing dramatically from a simple production line turning out two types of soap, Dominica Coconut Products now produces international brand names such as Dial, Imperial Leather and Palmolive for the entire Caribbean market. Edible oil, bottled and in bulk, as well as detergents and, most recently, cosmetics are other by-products of the raw coconut crop.

A Geest Line 'banana boat' arrives off Roseau to collect its weekly load of bananas for the United Kingdom

Dominica is the main supplier of fresh citrus to the Eastern Caribbean. Small traders organise their own marketing and shipping links with buyers in the neighbouring islands which have few agricultural products of their own, but need Dominica's fruit and flowers for their expanding tourism sectors.

Private sector involvement is the key to agricultural activity on this free enterprise island. Citrus growers operate their own packing plant for shipment of the grapefruit crop while a government-owned processing plant crushes and concentrates lime and grapefruit juice for export. The local market is supplied with bottled fruit juices by a small family company, Bello Products.

The Ministry of Agriculture is seeking to expand the processing potential of the citrus industry. The ministry is keen to attract investment from companies which would can and bottle juice locally, as well as those in North America and Europe interested in purchasing raw juice in bulk.

Vegetable and root crops are other products with potential. Already Dominica is in the forefront of supply to the Caribbean market but is looking towards opening up non-traditional outlets in the United States and Canada catering to ethnic groups and the growing general interest in Creole Caribbean cuisine.

Off-season supplies of temperate climate vegetables are also possible in the cool upland farms on the island. At these elevations, between 1000 and 2000 feet above sea level, strawberries, cauliflower, broccoli and the like are easily cultivated throughout the year.

This location is also ideal for the growth of exotics, ornamental foliage and cut flowers. The agricultural department is particularly interested in securing markets for the wide variety of plants produced. Anthuriums and ginger lilies, orchids, bromeliads, ferns and any number of broad-leafed creepers and variegated succulents are readily available.

Dominica is within two hours' flying time of the United States mainland and the intention is to develop airline links for the speedy transportation of these fruit, vegetables and exotic ornamentals. The government and National Development Corporation (NDC) look forward to discussing possible service operations with air cargo companies interested in the Dominica to United States route.

The cultivation of coffee and cocoa has been long established here. French planters were the first to establish coffee plantations over two hundred years ago. Since then coffee has always had mixed fortunes but has remained a standard crop regardless of the fluctuating markets. Now there are new opportunities for coffee and a major boost has been given to its cultivation over the last five years by a foreign aid sponsored tree crop programme which has encouraged farmers to upgrade their old fields and increase propagation. The wet hillsides of Dominica are ideally suited to this crop.

The Bello Products Company which also manufactures the fruit juices has just signed an agreement with government to purchase all the coffee which farmers can produce. This has given new confidence to the farmers and has enhanced the island's agro-processing base. Dominica coffee is favoured locally and regionally over other imported ground coffees and the aim is to move into the international market as a specialised product.

High quality spices and essential oils are another tradition of Dominican agriculture. Well-established stands of nutmeg, cinnamon and cloves are common on the mixed-crop farms in Dominica. These supply the local and regional export markets but are sold unpackaged, and there is scope for both local preparation and packaging as well as bulk exports to international purveyors of spice products.

Essential oils from patchouli, West Indian bay leaf and citronella grass, which form the base materials for perfumes, are also produced but are in urgent need of a larger market. Traditional buyers are quickly glutted and particularly in the case of bayleaf oil, the island can produce far more than its usual purchasers require. Here again there is a ready opening for new buyers and processors. One US company, Windward Islands Aloes Ltd., runs a well established aloe farm and processing operation which is a fine example for other interested investors.

The abundance of fresh water flowing from Dominica's many rivers not only nurtures the fertile soil and provides water for export to the drier islands, but is also harnessed for fish farming. A Taiwanese assisted project is already harvesting quantities of freshwater prawns from ponds fed by one of the larger streams. In another part of the island Australian freshwater lobsters are being reared under similar conditions. The sections of flat land along the larger river valleys are ideal for the development of fish farming which demands little more infrastructure than the excavation of ponds along the river banks.

Agriculturally, Dominica is one of the last islands in the Caribbean still open to pioneers. Individual investors or corporate entities can have the choice of sharing any number of completely new ventures or of tapping into the existing farming sector at any level of the production line either as a cultivator, processor, exporting agent or purchaser and distributor on the international market.

To back up that investment is an efficient government agricultural department with extension officers in touch with all areas of the farming community. The National Development Corporation assists with pioneer-industry incentives and guidelines. The private enterprise body, the Dominica Association of Industry and Commerce (DAIC) provides contacts and potential partners in the business sector eager to welcome new colleagues to participate with them in the development of this fertile island.

Launching an inter-island trading sloop at Toucari Beach, the Dominican flag flying proudly from the wheelhouse *(opposite)*

| 5 |
Fishing

Although fishing makes an important contribution to local food production, there are few full-time fishermen. Most go fishing only a couple of days a week and farm the rest of the time. Scotts Head, Fond St Jean, Anse-de-Mai, Calibishie, Vieille Case and Marigot are the main fishing villages. The majority of west coast fishermen only do fishing with seine nets. There is always a demand for fish but the supply is limited. A sudden traffic jam on a coastal road may signal the arrival of a boat with a catch of fish as drivers park haphazardly to join the crush around the boat. There is a very distinctive way of advertising the sale of fish by blowing conch shells to let the neighbourhood know that fish is available. The villagers then gather by the landing place to exchange news and see what luck the boats have had.

Among the most popular fish for eating are Dorado or Dolphin fish, King fish, Tuna, Bonito, Snapper, Cavali and Flying fish. Jacks and Balaou are favoured for making a 'fish braff' or clear stew. These are caught in long nets either hauled in a circle by two canoes or surrounded close to shore and pulled up in the nets by helpful passers-by who share in the catch.

The Caribs once used bows and arrows to shoot fish near the surface of the water. In the rivers various poisons were also used. One was *nivwage* which was made from the pounded leaves of the bush of that name. This was thrown into small pools and as the fish began to jump from the water to escape the effects of the poison they were seized. Another poison was made from the *bambarra* fruit which was crushed, placed in a basket and put in the water so as to stun the fish. The bark of the *bwa savonette, bwa sisserou* and *bwa pipiri* were also used as poisons. Like the use of dynamite for fishing, these poisons have been made illegal.

Besides sea fishpots, *nas*, there are also small basket fish traps for river crayfish. Crayfish are also caught by tying a piece of vine or *caapi* to a rock and passing the other end of the vine through a piece

Nets drying at Douglas Bay *(opposite)*

Fishing boats returning home at Marigot (DR PETER EVANS)

of coconut or *manioc*. Fishermen come at night to catch the crayfish nibbling at the bait.

Fishermen can judge the right times to go fishing off rocks along the shore. Many of these places are reached only by dangerous paths along the sea cliffs. Such fishing is best done at the cooler times of day 'when the fish rise' or at night with *flambeaus* to attract the fish.

When fishing by boat men usually go in groups of three or four. For a trip into the 'canal' or channel between the islands, they usually leave at sunrise and return about 4.00 pm. To see these brave men *en canal* is quite an experience as they confidently handle boat and fishing-tackle while their small craft appears and disappears among the great swells coming in from the Atlantic Ocean. The fish are all caught with hook and line, although the larger types often require a harpoon. Flying fish, *volant*, are an exception, for when the schools are large a *kali*, made of bamboo basketing is used to scoop the fish aboard. Back on shore, the day's catch is shared in the traditional way between the owner of the boat and other fishermen.

The calmer West Coast is the area most popular for net fishing using *seines*. To sight a school of jacks, bonik or balaou is to claim it. Often one sees canoes going out with a pile of seines in the stern and straw *pai* in the bows. The straw is used to 'fe pai', that is to spread the straw on the water so as to attract fish such as *balaou* which surface to play with it. Sometimes one sees as many as ten or more boats waiting for a large school of balaou or bonik which has been seen in a certain area. In such a case the fishermen have their own traditional agreements as to who gets a chance to set their seine first, in which order and where, since various claims are made on schools of fish depending on who sighted it or was the first to 'fe pai'.

The latest form of shore fishing is with the spear-gun. Generally these are homemade copies of the imported spear-gun, using a wooden handle, car-tyre rubber and a sharpened length of iron reinforcing rod. Using goggles, the spear men scour the reefs and rocks and in many cases completely out-fish certain areas, leaving hardly anything for the fishermen standing on the rock. Spear-guns have had the same effect on river fishing.

| 6 |
The tropical forest

The high backbone of mountains which runs along the centre of Dominica from north to south, cuts straight across the path of the north-east Trade Winds sweeping in from the Atlantic Ocean. The average height of the mountainous central range is about 3,000 feet and it forces the high level winds to rise long before they reach the island. Moist air and heavy clouds are formed by this action over the sea and east coast, and rain-showers fall along the windward side as well as on the mountains themselves. On reaching the west or leeward coast the air has lost most of its moisture, resulting in a dry 'rain shadow' coastline. Sharp variations of temperature, caused by altitude, also create different micro climates which, linked to the rainfall pattern, determine which species of plant will grow in which area. Rainfall figures in Dominica range from an average of 50 inches per annum, along the driest west coast stretch, to 300 inches in the central range.

Diagram of the tropical forest

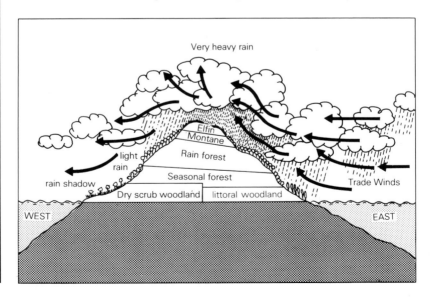

All these factors have combined to give us roughly six different types of forest. Along the east and north coasts, we find the **windward littoral woodland**, including the **swamp forest**; on the west coast, the **dry scrub woodlands**; going higher, we find the **seasonal or deciduous forest**; then between 500 and 2,000 feet we get into the **rain forest**; higher still is the **cloud forest**, made up of **montane forest** and around the peaks of the highest mountains the **elfin woodland**.

Windward littoral woodland

Along the breezy windward coast, from the back of Scotts Head in the south and up around the north-east to as far as Cape Melville or Capucine Point, there runs a belt of shrubby vegetation swept back by the wind, clipped as if shaped by some giant brush; it is a sort of elfin woodland at sea level. The dominant species are Raisin bord-de-mer, Ziquaqe or 'fat pork', and Bois Chandelle. The large trees are made up of West Indian White Cedar or Poirier, West Indian Almond *Terminalia catappa*, Galba *Calophyllum antillanum* and Gommier l'incence *Rhus metopium*.

'Mang' trees in the swamp forest (CAROL KANE)

Swamp forest

Because there are so few marshy lowland sites on an island where the coastline is very precipitous there are very few examples of the common mangrove. Swamp areas are dominated by the buttressed tree, *Pterocarpus officinalis*, known locally as 'mang'. These fringe the sluggish river mouths such as the Indian River, Anse de Mai, Hodges and Woodford Hill. In open swamp areas, the Cabrits and Glanvillia for instance, there are varieties of sedge, large ferns including *Acrostichum daneaefolium*, and semi-woody arums.

Dry scrub woodland

The leeward coast is, by Dominican standards, a hot, dry, stony shoreline. The mountains behind, which take most of the rain, also block out the cooling breezes and at mid-afternoon, the sun in the western sky and its glare from the sea, combine to raise temperatures even higher. Grand Savanne, situated at the widest part of the island is consequently also the driest part. Here, rough grass and hardy scrub survive on the very shallow soil and over four varieties of cactus grow from the cliffs. The dominant trees along this side of the island from Scotts Head to Capucine are: Logwood, known locally as Campeche, once exported in large quantities as dye; the mauve flowered Savonette *Lonchocarpus latifolius*, and Peeling Indian or Gommier Rouge *Bursera simaruba*. This coast is the natural habitat for our national flower, the ox-blood red Bois Caribe *Sabinea carinalis*. The giant trees of this zone are the Coubari *Hymenaea courbaril*, which provide excellent furniture wood, and the impressively buttressed Silk Cotton tree or Formager *Ceiba occidentalis* which, from the time of the Arawaks, has been associated throughout the Caribbean with the spirit world.

Seasonal or deciduous forest

Moving from the varied coastlines, we rise into the semi-evergreen type of forest which rings the whole island. This level is also the most heavily cultivated, and therefore most of the trees will be found on the steeper slopes, or between farms and fields. The most common types are Anglin *Andira inermis*, Caconier *Ormosia monosperma*, Acajou *Cedrela odorata*, Petite Feuille *Myrica splendens*, Mahaut piment *Daphnosis caribaea* and the Bois Tan or

Moricypre *Byrsonima spicata*. One of the showiest local orchids *Epidendrum ciliare* occurs within this zone. The dominant tree along the river banks is the massive broad-leafed Bois Riviere *Chimarrhis cymosa*.

The rain forest

The most luxuriant and extensive of all the forest formations in Dominica is the tall broad-leafed evergreen rain forest generally found at altitudes between 1,000 and 2,500 feet. Rain forest is the optimal formation in the tropics and, according to one of the most acknowledged U.S. experts on tropical vegetation, W H Hodge: *Nowhere in the American Tropics can a better display of it be seen than in the interior of Dominica*. Because of the rate of deforestation elsewhere it is one of the last oceanic or island-based rain forests in the world. The high rainfall and difficulty of access by man, maintain and protect it. However, extension of roads and farms over the last thirty years has reduced its area by thousands of acres, particularly in the large Layou Valley basin and on the north-eastern foothills of Morne Diablotin.

Like the island itself, the rain forest is composed of a number of distinct layers, each with its own delicately balanced micro-climate, supporting hundreds of plant and insect species. In the highest emergent layer, the lofty crowns of the tallest trees rise above the canopy, taking the most light, rain and wind. These giant trees like the Gommier *Dacryodes excelsa*, provide flowers, fruit and shelter for bees, parrots and smaller birds, including the humming birds and the Rufous-throated Solitaire or Siffleur Montagne.

At a slightly lower level is the main forest canopy. Rain and sunlight filter through this cover some 100 feet above the forest floor. The top sides of the wettest branches are hanging gardens of orchids, bromeliads, ferns, mosses and other plants whose roots never touch the soil. Floor-based lianas climb to the canopy to get sunlight. Dominant trees include the Balata *Manilkara bidentata*, Carapite *Amanoa caribaea* and Chataigner *Sloanea* spp as well as the Gommier.

In the dark understorey, palms, tree ferns and thin trees stretch upwards in search of scarce sunlight. This is the most active layer

Gommiers in the rain forest at Syndicate (DR PETER EVANS) *(overleaf)*

for moths and hundreds of species of insect. The shadowy forest floor is covered with seedlings starting their long journey upwards. Termites, fungi and bacteria feed on the layer of fallen leaves decomposing on the ground, creating nutrients which are quickly absorbed by the root systems of the trees above.

Dominica's many rivers depend on these forests for their survival. Clean, filtered water seeps beneath the forest floor into streams supporting a variety of fish and crustacea, including crabs and crayfish. Wherever the forest is cut, one notices how fast the tiny streams which feed the main rivers dry up. This is the result of being exposed to the sun and losing the sponge-like root and soil system which slowly but constantly releases water into the streams.

Hurricane David in 1979 wrought havoc upon the rain forest in the south and central parts of the island, stripping away the canopy and tossing about giant trees like matchsticks. Regrowth was amazingly swift, but without the canopy the true character of the rain forest in these areas has not yet been restored. The best examples of rain forest intact are in the Northern Forest Reserve, particularly on the northern and western slopes of Morne Diablotin.

Montane forest

After reaching 2,000 feet, the rain forest gradually gives way to shorter, thinner trees, interspersed with mountain palm, palmiste. At about 2,500 feet this montane forest or thicket, as it is sometimes called, is supreme. We are in the cloud forest, a windy, misty, dripping world where tree trunks and branches are draped in moss and filmy ferns cover the soggy forest floor. The main trees here are Bois Rouge *Cyrilla racemiflora*, Raisinier Montagne *Podocarpus coriaceus* and Bois Bande *Richeria grandis*

Elfin woodland

From 3,000 feet upwards to the peaks of the highest mountains, the trees become more stunted and gnarled. A combination of high winds from the easterly trades, little or no soil (except for spongy humus), and temperatures between 60 – 65°F throughout

A giant tree fern frames the southern peaks (from left to right) of Morne Watt, Morne John and Morne Anglais *(overleaf)*

The non-indigenous lobster claw Heliconia (DR PETER EVANS)

the day and lower in the nights and rainy months, all combine to create this dwarfed woodland. The foliage has a windshorn, clipped appearance. The twisted trunks, branches and aerial roots are so intertwined that it is often easier to clamber across the treetops rather than to try to touch the ground. The atmosphere is almost completely saturated.

The most common plants here are the Kaklin *Clusia venosa* and Gumbo Montagne *Hibiscus tulipaeflorus*. Two montane level palms are present – the *Euterpe globosa* and *Geonoma hodgeorum*. A splash of colour is given by the *Heliconia bihai*, and several species of anthurium, particularly the *dominicense* and the *grandifolium*. There are 2 – 300 epiphytes and bromeliads and ferns are thick upon the rocks and branches. Here you get a hint of alpine blossoms with the purple flowers of the *Tibouchina cistoides*, a dwarf shrubby melastome.

On the summits of the highest peaks one often finds several square feet of rocky exposed ground which have too little soil to support any bushes, yet the moisture supports pioneering herbs, including mosses, short ferns and ground level bromeliads. At this point, one has traversed the entire botanical range in Dominica, from the seashore to almost 5,000 feet. As an exercise in both stamina and botany, there are two mountains which it would be possible to scale in one day, starting from the sea. One could hike up Morne Anglais, starting from Castle Comfort along the track which leads past Giraudel or, even more challenging, up Morne Diablotin, starting at Pointe Ronde and using the old feeder road to Syndicate, before joining the track to take one up the last 3,000 feet.

| 7 |
Wildlife

As is typical of oceanic islands, the wildlife in the forests of Dominica is limited to small animals, with birds predominating. The island's distance from the mainland continent of South America and the effects of winds and ocean currents on the distribution and migration of wildlife from the mainland is the reason for this. Lying roughly 15.5° north of the Equator, Dominica is in the path of the south equatorial current. This flows from West Africa to South America, where a branch of it mingles with fresh water coming from the Orinoco River and then flows up along the southern Caribbean. The arrival of our first plants and seeds depended on this current, and to a great extent was responsible for the introduction of wildlife.

The flood waters of the Orinoco brought down matted weed beds and giant trees, which were then swept along by the current system and floating drift. It brought us our varied insect and reptile life, including the five species of non-poisonous snake, various lizards and frogs. Although our small mammal, the *Agouti*, and the marsupial *Manicou* or opossum originally came from the mainland, it is believed that they were brought later by man.

The movement of birds up the islands was much easier. The native parrots, for example, came upon Dominica by chance and gradually, after thousands of years of isolation, these Amazonas developed characteristics which were uniquely their own. In other cases, species may have changed elsewhere, through adaptation, but on Dominica birds such as the larger *Sisserou*, have remained in their primitive form. Some birds and animals arrived to find that they had to adapt to new types of predators, while others were suddenly in a paradise with no predators at all. New food chains settled into place and when Man arrived a few thousand years later, the wildlife of Dominica had fully adapted itself to its new island home.

Sisserou (DR PETER EVANS) *(above left)*   **Humming bird** (DR PETER EVANS)*(above right)*

Birds

There are roughly 166 species of bird at various elevations and habitats throughout the island, with the middle elevations being the most populated. The monarchs of the rain forest are of course the *Sisserou* or Imperial parrot (*Amazona imperialis*) and the *Jacko* or Red Necked Parrot (*Amazona arausiaca*). The Sisserou is the National Bird and appears on the flag, coat of arms and ceremonial Mace used in the House of Assembly. Its name has been adopted by many products from hotels to manufactured goods. There has been great concern in recent years about the declining numbers of these birds and their protection has been the key concern of the Forestry and Wildlife Division. They are totally protected by law, but there is a constant threat from loss of habitat through deforestation for agriculture and the devious monetary temptations offered by illegal collectors in Europe and North America.

Another distinctive bird is the *Siffleur Montagne* or Mountain Whistler whose tremulous, rather mournful call echoes like a four-note whistle across the cloud forest. Any amateur ornithologist will require more than this brief chapter to steer him through the details of our birdlife and the best references are *The Birds of the West Indies* by James Bond and *Birds of the Eastern Caribbean* by Peter Evans. The Forestry Division also has a number of slim publications on sale, which will give more information.

With these guides at hand, you will discover the Chicken Hawk or *Malfini*, which glides upon unseen spirals above the valleys, seeking out lizards and grass snakes; the *Rossignol*, which is happy to build nests along the eaves of country houses; or the *Trembleur* darting like a busy-body from branch to branch. The commonest birds are small finches with various Creole names and the sucrier or bananaquit, a yellow and black honey creeper. Humming birds are also common, some with purple throats and others with green caps, darting their long tongues into the depths of forest flowers or skimming along the top of elfin woodland. The rasping cackle of the *Coucou Manioc* or Mangrove Cuckoo will attract you to admire his brownish grey plumage with highlights of white and yellow. There are also two kinds of *Grive*, Scaly-breasted and Pearly-eyed Thrasher, the Forest Thrush in the rain forests and the *Gros Bec*, medium-sized birds that frequent the intermediate zone just below the rain forest. Then we have the acrobatic *Choeque* who often hangs upside down to peer under leaves for food. The chief game birds are the *Ramier* and *Pedrix*. The two main doves are the Zenaida Dove or *Toutwell* which inhabits lower elevations, and the Ground Dove or *Ortolan*, which flutters in short leaps from one spot to the next.

Along the river valleys we may spy the cautious Heron or *Crabier* searching for small crustaceans among the river rocks. The handsome Kingfisher flashes by, giving us a quick glimpse of his blue-grey feathers, chestnut breast and white fringes. Up in the hills at night we will be lucky to hear the reclusive owl. Even less likely, will be the sighting of the *Diablotin* bird, a black-capped petrel, long believed to be extinct, but which has been recently seen once more. These birds gave their name to the two northernmost mountains of Dominica, Morne Diablotin and Morne Aux Diables.

Along the seashore the spotted Sandpiper or *Baygas* walks and darts at the surging water's edge. Huge Frigate birds glide almost motionless, black against the sky. Tropic birds with their white scissor-tails nest in holes along the sheer cliff face, and the occasional Sea Hawk dive-bombs a shoal of fish. Only very rarely do we see the clumsy Brown Pelican, who prefers the reef-lined shores of the Leeward Islands. Our few wetland areas, at the Cabrits and Indian River swamps and at the Freshwater Reservoir, provide temporary habitat for several migrant birds travelling north and south across the Americas.

Fish

In the rivers, there are fish with names like *Mullet*, *Tayta*, *Dormi*, *Titiri* and *Kro-kro*. On the river-bed are crustaceans such as the Crayfish, called *Kribish*, and the smaller, shrimp-like *Bouk*. Upon the rocks cling the small edible snail we call *Vio*, and along the river banks the brown and yellow *Cyrique* crab scurries beneath the boulders. His other relatives, the White Crab and Black Land Crab prefer the coastal zone. These are the source of the Dominican Crab Back, served in most restaurants. The amusing Hermit or Soldier Crab changes its shell as it grows bigger. It likes to be close to rocky beaches where there is an abundance of discarded shells from which to choose a new home.

Reptiles

Among the reptiles there is the common *Zandoli*, and in the scrub forest the much larger, blue dotted *Abolo* lizard. The dragon-like, bright green Iguana is not all that common, and favours the hot west coast as its habitat. At night, the ugly Gecko lizards go on the prowl for insects. We call them *Mabouyas*, which is the same name given by the ancient Caribs to their evil spirits. Added to this, these geckoes

Mountain chicken (DR PETER EVANS)

41

cackle in a deep, ominous tone: 'cuk-cuk-cuk-cuk-cuk'.

Luckily, Dominica has no poisonous snakes, and three of the five species here are very small. The largest is the *Tete Chien*, a boa constrictor which can grow to eight feet long although most are about half that size. The mere sight of these strikes terror into the hearts of the majority of Dominicans, and there is a fanatic passion to kill them immediately. In fact, they do not attack unless aggravated. In all my years of walking the forest, I just divert slightly when coming upon them, and leave them alone.

The prize reptile is the Mountain Chicken, or *Crapaud*, an amphibious creature related to the toad whose fried or stewed legs are a national delicacy. It lives in areas below 1000 feet, but for some reason does not inhabit the northern or eastern parts of the island. The Crapaud comes out at night, and his constant 'prup-prup' can be heard above all the other night time calls. I have often thought that a Crapaud farm would be a very lucrative business, at the same time protecting those in the wild.

Insects

The insects are dominated by the Hercules Beetle. The giant male has a single claw at the top of its head, which could be mistaken for a crab's pincers. This helps him break up dry wood in search of grubs and termites. Other forest dwellers are brown and grey, broad-winged Moths. Skeletal stick insects called *Chuval-Bois* sit, disguised, on branches. Huge green Grasshoppers emit a 'crack-crack' sound which gives them their name. Then, there is the carnival of butterflies in hues of yellow, red, orange, brown, black and white. At night, large fireflies, which we call *La Belles*, perform a ballet of twinkling lights against the dark backdrop of the forest.

Mammals

Our four-legged forest dwellers are few. The Agouti is a large rodent, rather like a long-legged guinea pig, which criss-crosses the forest floor. The sluggish Opossum or Manicou leaves its tree-top hole at night to forage on the ground. Wild pigs roam the most inaccessible parts of the rainforest. They are the descendants of domesticated pigs brought here by the early European settlers and which took to the woods. Barbecued wild pig was a favourite feast for the

Agouti (DR PETER EVANS)

African Maroons who escaped into the hills in the Eighteenth Century.

All wildlife considered as game is protected by law, and can only be hunted during the declared open season from 1 September to 28 February. A paid permit is required from the Forestry Division. Total protection is given to all those birds not mentioned in the legislation as game birds including the two parrots which may not be hunted or taken on any account.

| 8 |
Roseau – tropical Victorian

Most Caribbean ports are clustered around sheltered bays and anchorages but Roseau, capital of Dominica, is by contrast situated on a gently rounded headland. It was chosen by the French as the site of their largest settlement because it provided the greatest expanse of flat land along the leeward coast and it was well supplied with fresh water from the nearby river. The French name for the town came from the profusion of river reeds, *roseaux*, which grew all about the estuary.

Geologically the town sits on a fan-shaped river delta made up of alluvial sand and boulders deposited by the Roseau River over the years as it meandered to and fro across the area. It is also composed of ash and pumice ejected thousands of years ago from the bowels of Morne Micotrin, which stands guard over the town at the head of the Roseau Valley. Visiting vulcanologists have made ominous remarks about the position of the town in relation to this dormant volcano, but having lived with it safely for five hundred years of recorded history few people give much thought to the moods of Micotrin.

The river itself changed course freely in the early days of colonisation, creating placid lagoons, one of which, though long since vanished, gave its name to the area of Roseau still known as Lagon today. As late as 1806 the river tried to regain some earlier course by bursting its banks, killing over 130 townspeople in the process. The construction of successive defensive walls has, however, tamed the roving instincts of the floodwaters which thunder down during the rainy season.

By about 1730, the original group of French huts had grown into a small village with its centre in the area of the Old Market Square. On the hill nearby a rough wooden fort was built to look out for the English and roving pirates. The haphazard growth of this settlement is still evident when you notice the narrow, crooked nature of the streets in this part of town.

When the British captured the island in 1761 and ceded it to their growing empire two years later, a formal survey was done and plans were laid out for streets and house lots on an orderly grid system. The final plan was drawn up by surveyor Nathanial Minshall in 1768. Today, therefore, it is easy to note the boundaries of the crooked old French Quarter and the British grid which extends from Cork Street to the River Bank.

The names of the streets also give us a hint of the historical period. Lord Hillsborough was then Secretary of the Board of Trade, the equivalent of the Colonial Secretary. Great Marlborough was still remembered for his victory at the Battle of Blenheim. Great George was King George III, monarch of the day, and Hanover was the Royal House of which he was a member. An attempt was made to change the name of Roseau to Charlotteville in honour of his wife, Queen Charlotte, but this never caught on. There was also an idea to shift the port to a more protected southerly location, thus creating a new town, but that did not succeed either, although the area is still called Newtown today.

The hub of the colonial government was positioned on the top of the hill which separates Roseau from Newtown. The stone fort (which replaced the wooden French one), Government House, the Court House and House of Assembly, the Anglican Church and Commissariat (the government offices) were all built within a few yards of each other.

Great George Street, Roseau (JAMES HENDERSON)

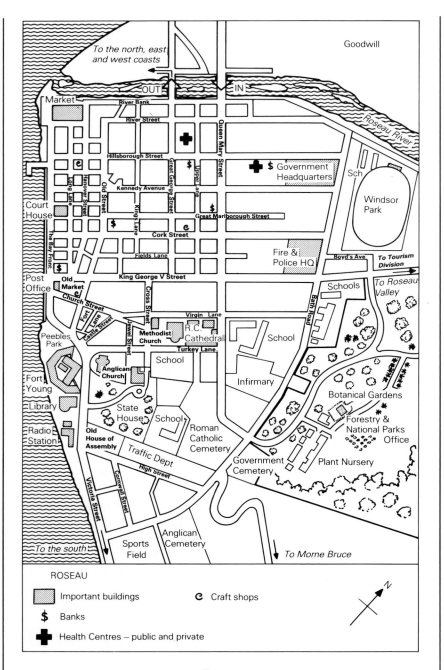

Roseau

Roseau has suffered from military action including bombardment, pillage and fire on three occasions: during the British capture in 1761; the French capture in 1778; and during another French attempt in 1805 when the entire town was destroyed by fire as flaming wadding from the cannons was blown by the wind and landed on the wood shingled rooftops. An earlier and similarly disastrous fire engulfed the whole town in 1781 during the French occupation. Several blocks have also been destroyed by fire from time to time over the last 100 years. Most of the town's earliest and best examples of architecture were lost during these conflagrations.

Hurricanes have also taken their toll. Roseau was hit and severely damaged by these storms in 1781, 1806, 1813, 1834, 1916, 1928, 1930 and 1979 with several lesser gales also battering the town between those years.

Most public utilities were introduced in the latter half of the nineteenth century. Piped water was brought in from Riviere Douce in 1874, the same year as the first bridge across the Roseau River was completed. The Roseau Town Board was established in 1896. Electric power was introduced in 1905.

Until 1979 the main anchorage and shipping place was along the Bayfront. The last steel and concrete pier was destroyed by Hurricane David and coincided with the move of the main port to the deepwater harbour at Woodbridge Bay.

Dominica was never a wealthy colony and this is reflected in her architecture. The capital claims distinction for its quaint wood and stone townhouses, most of which date from the Victorian period. These can be recognised by their overhanging verandahs decorated with fretwork, their jalousie louvres and heavy wooden shutters. Much has been lost in the old quarter of town through decay and some rather ugly replacements, but several good examples can still be seen in this area. The small scale of most of the buildings is a result of fragmented ownership since the 18th century, as blocks were sub-divided into smaller and smaller pieces so that today some travel writers comment on the miniature scale of the town. Thirty years ago, before the development of suburban housing areas, many more families lived in central Roseau. As they moved out, the town dwellings were converted into shops and offices.

Roseau is the hub of government, commerce, health services and education, communications and information. Getting anything done requires a visit to Roseau and every active farmer or businessman on the island usually has to visit the town at least once a week. Everything converges on the town during the week and on Saturday mornings, but at night and on weekends the thoroughfares are empty. Traffic chokes the narrow streets three times a day, at 8.00 am, 1.00 pm and 4.00 pm, as schoolchildren, workers and vendors arrive from the countryside and suburban villages, go to lunch and then disperse for the evening.

Roseau tour

Government Headquarters, popularly called the Ministry, stands at the top of Kennedy Avenue. The House of Assembly and the offices of all ministers of government are situated here. Various departments of those ministries are housed in other offices scattered around the town.

Police Headquarters, the control point for the 19 police stations around the island, is on the corner of King George V Street and Bath Road. The passport and immigration department has its office in this building.

The Court House and Registry building is on the Bayfront, facing out to sea. The Magistrates' Courts are on the ground floor, while the High Court meets upstairs during the Assizes held three times a year.

The General Post Office is further south along the Bayfront in one of the older buildings of Roseau, constructed as the Market House in 1810. It was later converted to include a large public clock which was so badly placed that you have to be out in a boat to see the clock-face properly! Stamps are sold upstairs, and there is a small philatelic bureau for stamp collectors. Parcel post is at the other end of the Bayfront.

The Old Market Square stands behind the Post Office. Until 1971 this was a colourful centre of commercial activity. *La Place*, as it was called in Creole, has had a dramatic history, dating from the earliest period of French colonisation. Vendors of vegetables, food and merchandise have crowded this cobbled square for centuries. Slave auctions, executions and public punishments were carried out here, and it has been the scene of some lively political meetings and rallies. In 1895, Dominican philanthropist Edward Sheriff Dawbiney left £500 in his will for the construction of a covered area. Recently this has been converted into stalls for the sale of handicrafts and snacks, benches have been placed around the square and trees and flowers planted.

Climbing the hill to Victoria Street, you enter the old administrative centre. On your left is the **Cenotaph**, with two war memorials. The larger commemorates those who lost their lives in the two World Wars. The smaller one honours the Free French of the neighbouring islands, who made Dominica their base after the fall of France in 1940. **Peebles Park**, with its benches and bandstand, is on your right.

The St George's Anglican Church is directly ahead of you. It was built in 1820 in square Regency style, but early this century it was enlarged and converted into its present shape. It was totally destroyed by the hurricane in 1979, and suffered once again in its rebuilding.

Fort Young Hotel is directly opposite. Constructed in 1770 by the first British governor, Sir William Young, it was added to by the French between 1778 and 1783. After the 1850s it was used as a police station and was opened as a hotel in 1964. Destroyed by hurricane in 1979, it has recently been rebuilt and reopened. The Fort was the centre of action during the French invasions of 1778 and 1805 and though much of the historic fabric has been smothered in the concrete necessary to accommodate hotel bedrooms, one can still get a hint of the line of its ramparts and recall its turbulent past.

State House, formerly Government House, stands in the large garden across from Fort Young. From 1840 to 1979, it was the office and residence of the Governors, Administrators and Presidents of the island. A previous government house, constructed in 1766, once stood in the centre of the lawn. The present building has been converted for use as a venue for state receptions and for similar affairs organized by community groups. Apartments upstairs are for visiting dignitaries.

The ruins of the **Old Court House** stand sadly desolate further along Victoria Street. This once handsome building, constructed in 1811 in classical Georgian style, was burnt by arsonists on 16 June 1979 during political troubles. Hopefully one day it will be restored.

The jumble of concrete boxes across the street are the studios of the **Dominica Broadcasting Service**, unfortunately totally out of character with the architecture in the rest of this area. DBS broadcasts daily from 6.00 am to 10.00 pm, providing a vital link for the scattered villages and Dominicans in the neighbouring islands. Key programmes are the daily news, community and family announcements and what's on in entertainment.

The Public Library and **Victoria Memorial Building**, are also situated on this side of the street. The small Victoria Memorial built in 1902 in memory of the Queen Empress was once our museum but is now part of the DBS offices. Across the lawn is the Public Library constructed with a grant from the Scottish-American philanthropist Andrew Carnegie in 1906. It is heavily used by children and students, and houses the best sources of general information related to the history, social patterns, flora and fauna of Dominica. The first Public Gardens on the island once existed in the Library grounds but only the fascinating Cannon Ball Tree next to Fort Young remains today as evidence of this.

The Botanical Gardens form the eastern boundary of the town of Roseau, tucked beneath the verdant slopes of Morne Bruce. The first steps towards the establishment of these gardens were taken in 1889 at a time when the Crown Government wished to encourage the diversification of crops and provide farmers with correctly propagated seedlings. The site, covering some forty acres, once

The Botanical Gardens

planted in sugar cane, was sold to the government by William Davies, owner of Bath Estate in 1892. The first curator was Charles Murray of the Edinburgh Botanic Gardens. He was followed soon afterwards by Henry F Green, who began laying out and planting the grounds. In 1892, Joseph Jones took over what was to become for him a lifelong vocation.

The function of the Botanical Gardens was strictly of an economic and experimental character with ornamental plants grown to make the grounds attractive and interesting. The Gardens were closely linked to the Royal Botanic Gardens at Kew, and it was Kew which provided the exotic plants collected from every part of the tropical world. Up to the 1930s the Botanical Gardens of Dominica ranked among the finest in the West Indies, but many of the most impressive old trees were lost during Hurricane David. Yet the grounds still provide one of the last open spaces for the citizens of Roseau and beautiful surroundings for cricket matches and state parades.

Morne Bruce is an ideal vantage point from which to get a birds-eye view of the entire town of Roseau and the Botanical Gardens. The adventurous and agile may wish to scale the summit of the plateau by way of Jacks Walk which climbs steeply up from a point at the corner of the Botanical Gardens near the Elmshall Gate. The more usual way up is to take the longer motorable route which starts at the southerly end of Bath Road.

Morne Bruce was once the main military garrison for troops defending Dominica. It was named after the British Royal Engineer James Bruce, who designed all of the original fortifications for the island. This site was one of Bruce's main interests and extensive plans were made for its defence. The cliffs and steep slopes which surround it on three sides made it a natural post for the protection of Roseau. The old garrison graveyard still exists at Kings Hill on the way to Reigate Hall Hotel, and the Morne is reputed to have its own resident ghost, a headless drummer who marches with muffled drumbeat at midnight. The government still owns the top of the plateau, and the eighteenth century barracks are still used as the police training centre and government residencies. The best views of Roseau are obtained from beneath the giant crucifix and shrine which overlooks the town. This was erected in the 1920s, and one local wit at the time, who was no friend of the head of the diocese, commented that the shrine reminded him of the Bishop's mind: *A lot of spikes and very little Jesus!*

The Roseau Cathedral of Our Lady of the Assumption rises above the patchwork rooftops which crowd around the hill on which it stands, part of the low ridge which cuts across Roseau, from the Botanical Gardens to Fort Young. Like most Catholic churches in Dominica, the Cathedral started life as a thatched hut, built like the Carib Kabays of strong posts and woven palm leaves.

In all, it took over one hundred years to complete the Cathedral as we know it today, covering a period of stops and starts from about 1800 to 1916 when the small west steeple was completed. Made of cut volcanic stone, it was built in the style of Gothic-Romanesque Revival, very popular during the mid nineteenth century. Each section of the Cathedral has its story, each statue and altar has its own date of placement and blessing, and there is much to tell: funds raised by levies on French planters; the Caribs who camped outside Roseau for three months to erect the first wooden ceiling frame; the pulpit built by convicts on Devil's Island off Cayenne; the stained glass windows, one dedicated to Christopher Columbus; and the ornate Victorian murals behind the side altars.

The Methodist Church stands right next to the Cathedral on Virgin Lane. The position of this church and its Manse on the same block as the Cathedral is the result of an interesting twist of fate which dates back to May 1766 when King George III, recognising the importance of the French plantocracy on this recently captured island, granted the Catholics use of 10 acres in the town for 99 years for the benefit of their church. As this period of lease drew to a close, the Catholic Church appealed to the Crown for a freehold grant of these 10 acres. This was acceded to in 1865, except for two lots on the corner. These had been sublet to Catholics who had later converted to Wesleyan Methodism, and had made their lands available to the Wesleyan Mission. All is ecumenically peaceful now, but for years during the late 1800s there was great discomfort about their close proximity, which bubbled into an all-out street riot one night over a hundred years ago. Inside the Methodist Church are some interesting memorials, one of the most significant being to the memory of Charles Gordon Falconer one of the fiery leaders of the *Mulatto Ascendancy* in the nineteenth century.

The Roman Catholic Cathedral at Roseau built between 1800 and 1916 in the style of Gothic-Romanesque revival (MICHAEL BOURNE) *(opposite)*

The Public Market Place at the Roseau River mouth is the setting of a colourful human spectacle which is one of Roseau's main attractions. It is at its best early every Saturday morning, when truck-loads of farmers and country vendors arrive from the hills and spread their cornucopia of fruit, vegetables, root crops and flowers across the courtyards, sidewalks and stalls of the marketplace. This pageant has been performed for centuries through times of slavery and freedom, first at the Old Market Square across town, and since 1972 at this new site which even now is filled to overflowing on the busiest days. Those with an anthropological bent can have a field day amidst the crescendo of Creole patois and the hubbub of sale, barter and bargain, while observing the remnants of our West African culture in the manner of displaying produce in heaps and patterns on the ground rather than in restrictive upright stalls.

One of the houses of interest is the birthplace of the novelist **Jean Rhys** (1890 – 1979). Situated on Cork Street it is now Vena's Guest House. The garden, opening on to Fields Lane is now the World of Food Restaurant, a cool oasis in the shade of a giant mango tree.

Handicraft Shops are dotted around the capital. The long established Dominica Handcrafts is just down Hanover Street from the marketplace, and sells a variety of grass and Carib work as well as spices and local condiments. Caribana Handcrafts specialises in

Jean Rhys' house, now Vena's Guest House (MICHAEL BOURNE)

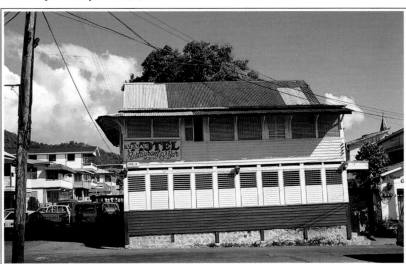

Carib baskets and has the best choices in Roseau of these traditional Amerindian handicrafts. Look out for the famous Dominican vertiver grass rugs and mats. Purchased readymade or made to order, they come in all sizes and designs and have a lovely crisp herbal scent when first purchased. Such mats have been Dominica's standard gift for British Royal weddings over the years, and they have always been much appreciated and put to immediate use. The two other main craft centres are at shops near the gates of the Deepwater Harbour and at the Old Market Square.

The Dominica Tourist Division provides maps of Roseau with more detailed information as to the whereabouts of banks, restaurants, the Cable and Wireless Office, clinics, doctors' offices and other services within the town. The Division is part of the National Development Corporation which has its head office next to the Bath Estate bridge. The central Tourism Information booth is in the Old Market Plaza.

| 9 |
Roseau Valley tour

There are interesting sights in the heights of Roseau Valley which, though not within the boundaries of the National Park, are closely associated with it. The Valley Road through Bath Estate branches out to three villages: Laudat, Trafalgar and Wotton Waven. The Laudat road takes you to the National Park, the lakes and the Titou Gorge; Trafalgar road takes you to the waterfalls; Wotton Waven road takes you to the Sulphur Springs.

Climbing past the village of Trafalgar you get your first view of the tops of the Trafalgar Falls, cascading side by side out of the deep gorges which they have carved for themselves. The motorable road stops at the hydro-electic power station and you then walk up the trail past Papillote mountain lodge and restaurant until you arrive at the viewpoint above the river. To your left is the tallest waterfall which some guides from the village like to call the 'father'; to your right is the shorter 'mother' fall. Others prefer to call them 'the male' and 'the female'.

The 'father' comes from the Freshwater Reservoir by way of Titou Gorge and the volume of water therefore fluctuates depending on how much is being taken off for the power plant. At its base, hot, iron-filled orange water pours out of cracks in the black rocks. Climbing up to the pool at its base, over the large, slippery boulders, is dangerous. Also beware of flash floods during heavy rains. At least one visitor has been lost, swept away by a sudden surge of flood water during the rainy season.

The 'mother' fall comes from deep in the heart of the National Park over the hill from the Boiling Lake, and is the end of the Breakfast River tributary. The water is colder, clearer and more constant than that of the other fall, and there is a lovely deep pool at its base which also requires some balancing and clambering skills to get to.

On the way back you may wish to call in at Papillote for a meal or drink. Papillote also has the best private botanical gardens on

Food crops surround houses near Roseau (CAROL KANE) *(opposite)*

57

Exhausted, but happy hikers enjoying the recuperative effects of both hot and cold water at the Titou Gorge

the island, specializing in rainforest orchids and bromeliads from the jungles of Dominica and South America. Among the bromeliads you will find *Pitcairnia angustifolia* with its slender, arching stems culminating in a spiky, brilliant red flower. Another, the *Nidularium innocentii*, with its central pink-tinted leaves, is an oasis in the rainforest offering a cup-sized pool of water at its centre for tree frogs, birds and insects. There is also a comprehensive collection of heliconias in combinations of red, yellow and green. Among the aroids is the rare *Anthurium dominicense* which comes from the remote Valley of Desolation.

For those not able or eager to do the Boiling Lake hike, you can visit miniature versions of the fumaroles and hot springs of the Valley of Desolation, by taking the road to Wotton Waven. You stop in the centre of the village, and take a track bordered by ginger lilies, to a bridge. From here you can see hot springs bubbling and steaming along the river bed and, further on, dotted across the cow pasture, are mud pools coughing and spluttering. This site has been studied for possible geothermal energy.

The main roads which wind along the steep sides of the Roseau Valley offer spectacular views of the rugged landscape. Tree-ferns and bamboos arch over the road, and from windows through the thick foliage you look down onto the silver threads of streams or across to mountains in the distance. From the plateau village of Morne Prosper, off the road to Wotton Waven, you get a panoramic view of the main mountains of the National Park.

There is a regular bus service to and from Trafalgar village on weekdays. Buses have no set schedule, but leave Roseau from a point at the bottom of Valley Road just up from Police Headquarters.

| 10 |
Trois Pitons National Park

Because Dominica has been so lavishly blessed with the natural assets of fertile soil, clean sources of water, rain forests, spectacular mountains and coral reefs, its inhabitants generally take their continuous provision for granted. Recently, however, concern has increased about ensuring that water catchment areas are protected, waste disposal is controlled and the precipitous landscape of the central mountains is protected from erosion caused by deforestation. With the population concentrated along the coast, it has been possible to promote the conservation of the central range which is, in fact, the storehouse of water and forest lands for the villages below.

An active forestry department spearheaded by British assistance in the 1940s was the embryo for the establishment of legislation and systems for the proper control of the ecology of the island. Forest reserves were surveyed in the northern and central mountain massifs and a system of forest guards and rangers was established. In the 1960s, international and local concern over better systems for preserving the environment led to interest in organising a national parks system.

Then in July 1975, after two years of boundary studies, surveys and legal preparation, the House of Assembly passed the National Parks and Protected Areas Act establishing a 16,000 acre National Park.

The Canadian Nature Federation, with the backing of the Canadian International Development Agency (CIDA) and with co-operation from Parks Canada, the National Museum of Natural Sciences and the Canadian Federal Justice Department, assisted in setting up the **Trois Pitons National Park**. The American owner of Springfield Plantations Ltd, John Archbold, donated another section of forest to be attached to the park as the Archbold Preserve. The park development plan concentrates on two elements: the maintenance of hiking trails, and the interpretation of the environment, including signs, literature and guided tours to explain the park to students and visitors.

Six trails exist along with picnic and rain shelters. The three most popular visitor sites are the **Emerald Pool, Freshwater Reservoir** and the less accessible **Boiling Lake**. In spite of pressing economic and social problems on the island, the creation of the Trois Pitons National Park and, eleven years later, the Cabrits National Park, both represent the strong conservation commitment of the staff of the Forestry and National Parks Department and of this young country as a whole. Dominica was the first of the Commonwealth Caribbean countries to establish a National Park. Potential returns from short term alternative uses of the land have given way to long term benefits and a modest nature-oriented tourism industry.

Access to the Park is gained by three routes: the **Laudat Village road** for trails to Freshwater Reservoir, Boeri Lake, Boiling Lake, East Coast Lookout, Grand Fond trail, Morne Micotrin and Morne Watt. The **Cochrane Village road** gains access to the Middleham Falls trail, including the Stinking Hole. This trail makes a loop to come out near Laudat. The third point is at the extreme north of the Park, on the Pont Cassé to **Castle Bruce road** for the Emerald Pool trail. The ascent to the summit of Morne Trois Pitons also starts in this northern section.

The entire Park is about the same size as the island of Carriacou in the Grenadines. Its name comes from the dominant volcanic massif which, when viewed from the west, does indeed appear to have three peaks, hence: *Trois Pitons*. The huge bulk of this mountain, reminding one of a titanic elephant at rest, rises to 4,600 feet. Damp, dripping montane forest and elfin woodland cover the entire massif and hide the fact that its surface is extremely rocky, with hardly a foot of topsoil upon the volcanic 'hard-pan' and boulders. These particular forest types thrive on the heavy rainfall and quick decomposition and absorption of nutrients.

Most of the Park is covered in these two types of cloud forest. This is because about 80% of the Park is well above the altitude favoured by true Tropical Rain Forest, which thrives between 1000 and 2,500 feet above sea level.

Moving south of Morne Trois Pitons, we come to **Morne Micotrin**, 4,006 feet high. The French called it Morne Macaque, but their reason remains a mystery for monkeys are not native to Dominica and there is no evidence of domestic monkeys having gone wild in that area. The original Carib name – Micotrin – has survived and is more commonly used today.

Micotrin and its surrounding lakes are part of a whole volcanic unit which had its birth about 5 million years ago. One of the greatest eruptions ever to have rocked the Caribbean occurred, creating a crater one and a half miles wide. Eventually, the whole cauldera began to resemble a teacup turned upside down onto a saucer. Micotrin was the teacup and the old crater, the saucer. A few million years later we find the two lakes caught in the lip of the saucer, Boeri Lake and the Freshwater Reservoir. Standing on the road above the Freshwater Reservoir you can still see the worn edges of the old crater forming an arc to the south.

Standing in the same position, you can also see the sharp humpback of **Morne Nicholls** (2,965 feet) and the tall pinnacle of **Morne Watt** (4,017 feet). Both are named after the two men who, in March 1875, ventured to the Boiling Lake and made its existence known to the world. Dr Henry Nicholls, particularly, wrote articles for *The Times*, *Illustrated London News*, and *The Geographical Journal*, which recounted the strenuous hike in the tones of dramatic Victorian adventure, similar to exploring the Congo or reaching the source of the Nile.

Further south, one sees the gently sloping flanks of **Morne Anglais** tapering to a point 3,683 feet above the sea. The last one

Morne Watt, at 4,017 feet, one of Dominica's taller mountains

thousand feet of this mountain is within the Park boundary, and it can be climbed relatively easily, starting from the village of Giraudel. The last 100 feet to the summit are, however, extremely dangerous, if not impossible, depending on the condition of recent landslides. Let discretion be the better part of valour, and admire the spectacular panorama before you from the safety of the lower peak. Dominica is spread at your feet: Roseau appears like a tiny patchwork triangle and on a clear day you can see Martinique, Guadeloupe and, occasionally, Montserrat. Across to the east is the most southerly mountain in the National Park, the virtually inaccessible **Morne Perdu Temps**, 3,150 feet high.

Apart from the mountains, there are five other major natural sites within the Park. Starting from the north, there is the **Emerald Pool**. This small pool is fed by a delicate cascade which plunges off the edge of a fern-covered cliff. The trail which leads to and from the pool is the best and easiest introduction to the tropical rain forest, at a point where it gradually becomes montane forest. From the well-maintained trail, you will see hundreds of fine examples of ferns, undergrowth shrubs, lianas, epiphytes and tall pillar-like tree-trunks at close range. From two lookout points you can survey the forest canopy from above, and look down the Belle Fille Valley to the pounding surf on the east coast. Part of the trail follows the route of the old Castle Bruce road, dating from the eighteenth century and perhaps from the Caribs before that. The rough cobbles you may see were laid in 1828. Until 1965, this track was the only link by land between Castle Bruce and Roseau. Imagine the reluctant mule trains from the plantations, the burdened porters on their way from town and the sick being carried in hammocks through the dripping forest.

The start of the Emerald Pool trail is clearly marked along the side of the present motorable road to Castle Bruce, at a point about half a mile after the junction with the road to Rosalie and La Plaine. The closest refreshment stops to the Emerald Pool are the Bush Bar, a mile further on, and Mano's Wayside Shop near the Tarrish Pit.

The Middleham Falls is best reached from the village of Cochrane, although you can also venture there from a marked point on the Laudat road, or from Sylvania on the Imperial Road. The latter is the longest and most difficult trek. This tall, thin waterfall shoots down into a narrow cul-de-sac similar to a half-open funnel, at the bottom of which is a round, clear pool. Coming from Cochrane, one arrives at the top of the waterfall – so expect a steep, slithery climb down to the pool. Nearby is another less accessible waterfall called the **Fond England Falls**.

The Stinking Hole, which can be passed on the way to the falls, is exactly what the name implies. It is simply a deep crevice on the forest floor, a haunt for thousands of bats, whose smell, mixed with some subterranean sulphurous fumes, creates the far-from-pleasant aroma which pervades the spot.

The origins of the Boeri Lake and Freshwater Reservoir were described earlier, as part of the Morne Micotrin eruption. The **Freshwater Lake** used to look rather like a blot of spilt ink, as it had about four different fingers of water radiating at crooked angles. Since being dammed for use as a reservoir, its surface area and shape have changed. It is the source of the Roseau River, and also the subject of myths and legends. A single-eyed monster, with gem-like carbuncles, was said to reside there, as reported by historian John Davies in 1666. For centuries, it was also said to be bottomless, although it was actually only 55 feet deep. If you visit on a grey, misty day, when windswept vapours swirl across its dragon-green surface, you will forgive the storytellers for creating their far-fetched legends.

The two and a half mile stone road from Laudat village to the Reservoir is part of Dominican folk history. Until 1963, it was the only route to La Plaine and the other south-east coast villages. Innumerable stories are attached to the journeys along this Chemin L'Etang, and colourful folksongs recall the rain-drenched barefooted slog of it all. From the lookout point, high above the lake, you can turn eastwards and look down to Grand Fond and the coast at Rosalie. Hikers can continue walking down into the Rosalie Valley along the old track until they reach the village of Grand Fond. Here you meet the motorable road which takes you to the east coast.

The **Boeri Lake** trail leads off from the shores of the Freshwater Reservoir in a north-easterly direction around the back of Morne Micotrin. An easy one and a quarter mile walk will lead you up and over two sharp ridges to the rocky shoreline of the lake, at an altitude of about 2,800 feet.

According to the National Parks Service, Boeri Lake may be at least 117 feet deep and its almost circular surface covers an area of about four acres. While the Freshwater Reservoir is fed by hillside streams,

**The placid Freshwater Reservoir at its original level
with the summit of Morne Watt in the distance**

Boeri Lake is filled by rainwater and runoff. The level of the lake fluctuates according to the annual rainfall, and sometimes, depending on the severity of the dry season, the level may drop more than 25 feet below high-water mark. The level is normally at its highest between October and December, when water may be seen leaving the lake, via the eastern outlet. At other times, it seeps out through the rocky lake bed like water through a filter, and depends on the high rainfall so as to be regularly topped up.

During the dry season, the huge, slippery boulders on the lake shore are exposed. Hikers have to be extremely cautious here, since the boulders lie haphapzardly upon one another, with gaping crevices in between, and one false step may mean twisting an ankle or breaking a leg.

Recently visitors have seen major intrusions into this section of the Park, because the original Freshwater Lake and the outflows from the Boeri have become sources for our hydro-electric power stations. The 'Lake' was excavated, streams rechanneled and the water level raised by over 20 feet. The original Freshwater Lake is now being operated as a giant man-made reservoir.

The Boiling Lake and **Valley of Desolation** are reached by way of a narrow trail from Laudat, less than four miles long as the tape measures, but taking three to four hours to walk one way. The whole expedition requires a full day. It is only for the fit and agile, capable of using both arms and legs as a means of locomotion over every conceivable gradient of terrain. Good strong shoes are a prerequisite, and a small backpack containing the essentials in food and drink is advisable. If you are not going with people who have been there before, you should hire a guide. Arrangements should be made a day or two in advance, either through your hotel, the Tourist Board or the National Parks Service. The guides are usually villagers from Laudat, and I am afraid payment is a matter of bargaining, because the fee has not been standardized. It is usually EC $80.00 for up to four people with an extra charge for every person over that number.

The hike begins at Laudat, across canals channeling water for the hydro-electric power station and then across the mouth of the **Titou Gorge**. This dark, narrow, water-filled canyon winds along to the base of a waterfall. The powerful flow of the water, which is too deep for standing, makes this little diversion an adventure only to be tried by strong swimmers. Take something to float on for a more leisurely swim up the gorge. A hot cascade at the mouth of the canyon can also give pleasant relief to sore muscles after returning from the Boiling Lake hike.

Continuing on our way, we cross gently sloping forest land until we drop into the valley of the **Breakfast River** which is so called because hikers traditionally stop at this point for refreshment before continuing their journey to the Boiling Lake. Then the endurance test begins. Up and over the narrow ridgeback of **Morne Nicholls**, from the top of which you get your first glimpse of the vapours rising from the lake and a little further on a birds-eye view of the **Valley of Desolation**. Clambering over the side of a steep ravine, we enter the steaming, rumbling valley which, as the name implies, is rock-strewn and barren, except for hardy ferns and grasses. After walking down the valley, avoiding bubbling fumaroles, bursts of hot steam, soft clay landfalls and simmering pools of black, blue and yellow water, we rise again on the left bank to walk along another ridge.

Hot streams and sulphur springs in the
Valley of Desolation *(opposite)*

66

Swirling clouds of steam rising from the volcanic crater of the Boiling Lake usually obstruct a clear view of the grey bubbling surface of the lake itself

Then, through two more ravines, we get into open country.

Walking across a moonscape, a hard carpet of moss-covered clay, we round the final ridge and there is the **Boiling Lake**, hopefully rumbling restlessly within the steep walls of its crater. It has many moods and it is impossible to predict from one visit to the next what state it may be in. I have seen it languid as a pale green soup; surging like a grey, storm-tossed sea; or milk-white with a central swirl of foam rising every few seconds to lash out against the craggy shore.

William Palgrave, who visited the lake in 1876, just a year after the track to it was first cut, has given a description of this curious phenomenon which can hardly be improved:

Fenced in by steep, mostly perpendicular banks varying from sixty to a hundred feet high, cut out in ash and pumice, the lake rages and roars like a wild beast in a cage, the surface, to which such measurements as we could make assigned about two hundred yards in length by more than half the same in breadth, is that of a gigantic seething cauldron, covered with rapid steam, through which, when the veil is for a moment blown apart by a mountain breeze, appears a confused mass of boiling waters . . .

One tragedy at the lakeside is still remembered. In 1901, Wilfred Clive, a descendant of Clive of India, died, presumably by asphyxiation by poisonous gases, while trying to save his guide who had collapsed after being engulfed by fumes along the shoreline of the lake. In recent years two other hikers have suffered accidental death along The Boiling Lake route. One tried to find his way back to Roseau by himself and fell over Trafalgar Falls. Another diverted slightly from the track on Morne Nicholls and fell 150 feet into the ravine below. Others have gone off on their own into the forest and have been lost for days, causing the police to send out search parties and, in some cases, request helicopters from Martinique. Please be extra careful on the more treacherous paths. Remember that the knotted terrain and the forest which covers it are like a giant maze, or as one visitor put it: *A large wet green trap.*

The Cabrits as seen from Picard Beach *(overleaf)*

| 11 |
The Cabrits National Park

The Cabrits National Park on Dominica's north-west coast is one of the unique protected sites of its kind in the Caribbean. Stunning mountain scenery, tropical deciduous forest and swampland, volcanic sand beaches, coral reefs and the romance of a fortified 18th century garrison are linked together within the 260 acre park. The name 'Cabrits' comes from the Spanish, Portuguese and French word for 'goat' because sailors left goats to run wild on the headland to ensure fresh meat on future visits.

The spectacular headland of the Cabrits, formed by the twin peaks of extinct volcanoes, overlooks two of the island's finest beaches. The town of **Portsmouth** nestles among the palms along **Prince Rupert's Bay**, while to the north, **Douglas Bay** shelters fascinating coral reefs. The Park is surrounded on three sides by the sea, its forested slopes plunging sharply into the blue-green waters of the Caribbean. A freshwater swamp of ferns, grasses and trees, which connects the Park to the mainland, is the nesting place for herons and doves and hosts a variety of migrant bird species. All this is dominated by the volcanic massif of **Morne Diablotin** – Dominica's tallest peak. From viewpoints at the Cabrits Park one looks northwards to the French islands of Les Saintes and Guadeloupe across the channel.

Prince Rupert's Bay has a rich maritime heritage dating from prehistoric times when Amerindian seafarers arrived in their long canoes. After Columbus' second voyage in 1493 adventurers on ships of all nations used the bay to refresh their crews and trade with the Carib Indians for food after the long Atlantic crossing. Spanish treasure ships called regularly. British privateers and explorers, including Drake, Hawkins, John White and Richard Grenville, visited. Horatio Nelson called often. French corsairs and Dutch traders found shelter. Prince Rupert of The Rhine sojourned here. United States naval pioneer Decatur fought a duel on the beach. Confederate ships defied the Yankee naval blockade here. Massachusetts whalers used the bay as a depot for half a century. Ann Davidson, the first woman to cross the Atlantic single-handed made her landfall here, and all types of vessels bearing rovers, rogues, regiments and royalty have anchored in the placid waters of Prince Rupert's.

Part of Douglas Bay forms the marine section of the Park. Graceful coconut palms, sea grape and West Indian Almond trees offer shade along the beach for picnics. A marine underwater trail in the centre of the bay provides interesting snorkeling. The more adventurous can explore fascinating rock and coral formations under the cliffs at the north end of Douglas Bay or hire a village fishing boat for the short trip.

Prince Rupert's Garrison

Hidden beneath the lush vegetation which covers the Cabrits, are the picturesque ruins of one of the most impressive military sites in the West Indies. Constructed between 1770 and 1815, the fortified garrison contains over fifty major structures. This military complex defended the north of the island during the period of colonial conflict and protected naval vessels anchored in Prince Rupert's Bay to rest their crews and collect fresh fruit, wood and water.

Fort Shirley

Most of the construction was undertaken by the British, but significant additions were made by the French during their occupation of Dominica 1778 – 1783. Together they amassed a garrison comprising one fort (Fort Shirley), seven gun batteries, seven cisterns, powder magazines, ordnance storehouses, barracks and officers' quarters to house and provide for over 600 men on regular duty.

The buildings on the Cabrits, or Prince Rupert's Garrison as it was officially called, are constructed of the same volcanic stone found scattered all over the hillsides. Skilled slaves and poor white artisans chiseled and shaped the hard rocks into the required forms for arched lintels, window sills and cornerstones. Some softer, dull pink stone from quarries at Grand Savannah was used for framing doors and windows. All of the red clay bricks one sees in the arches of the powder magazines, bakery ovens or water cistern walls came from England, transported as ballast in the sailing ships and removed on arrival in the colonies for private purchase or government use.

The cement used to bind these walls throughout the garrison was made of coral limestone. Collected on the reefs nearby, chunks of coral were heated in kilns on the beach until the limestone turned to powder. This was then mixed with fine aggregate, water and some molasses to help bind it together. Except for the action of tree roots, this mortar has certainly stood the test of time for it has kept everything together through hurricanes and earthquakes for over two hundred years.

The most active periods at the Cabrits were during the American War of Independence, the French Revolution and the Napoleonic Wars. The Battle of the Saints, fought between the French and British fleets on 12 April 1782 occurred within sight of the ramparts of the Cabrits. Fort Shirley was the scene of the famous revolt of the Eighth West India Regiment, an Afro-West Indian unit which mutinied and took control of the garrison for three days in April 1802 in a protest against conditions there.

The Cabrits was abandoned as a military post in 1854 and the luxuriant forest immediately regained control, tearing walls apart and shattering fine masonry. Several iron cannons were removed but many were left scattered among the trees where they still lie today. The trails used by visitors to the Park were laid by military engineers over 200 years ago and lead through the valleys and along the hilltops to all the main defence posts and viewpoints. The cruiseship reception berth and car park are situated on the site of the original dock where warships and merchant ships landed troops and supplies for the garrison. The terraced stone causeway leads up to the main gate from which the trails begin.

A complete tour of the Park can take half a day. Wear sensible walking shoes and light clothes. Take along your swimsuit and a snack. A camera, binoculars, diving mask and snorkel will enhance your trip. A suggested route is to start from the Park entrance, visit Fort Shirley and the museum, the valley and Commandant's House, the Centre Battery at the top of the Inner Cabrit, and back down to the Douglas Bay Battery. Please do not remove any artifacts.

The Cabrits Park is part of the Dominica National Parks System. Its establishment in 1986 was assisted by numerous funding agencies in co-operation with the Eastern Caribbean Natural Area Management Programme (ECNAMP) of the Caribbean Conservation Association.

Indian River boat ride

The **Indian River** has its source in the foothills of Morne Diablotin, and before entering the sea it meanders for about a mile through low-lying swamp-land just south of Portsmouth. The Caribs lived

Inter-island trading sloops on the Indian River (DR PETER EVANS)

on the higher ground up-river, but used the estuary as a route to the sea. Early European sea captains who visited the bay for wood and fresh water knew it as 'the river of the Indians' and often rowed up to the settlement to offer greetings to the chief. Soon it was marked on the map simply as Indian River, but the Indians have long since gone.

What attracts attention now is the luxuriant vegetation hanging overhead and along the banks of the placid waters of this meandering stream. Its twisting course is made even more contorted by the serpentine roots of the grand Mang trees which cling to the bank. Ferns, lianas and reeds cluster between the trees and the narrower sections of the river forming a green tunnel of foliage. Herons break the silence and beady-eyed crabs shuffle between the roots. Fish occasionally break the surface and now and then showers of rain hiss down upon the thick canopy of leaves above. Disney World may have produced all this in fibre-glass, but here is the real thing – a miniature Amazon adventure.

Arranging for a boat ride up the river may be the toughest part of the trip. All around Prince Rupert's Bay potential boatmen will be hustling you to take a ride up the Indian River. Take your time; do not be ruffled. The best place to make your choice of boatmen and boat is at the Borough's Square, near to the old Portsmouth Jetty. Either you set off from there, or they arrange to meet you at the mouth of the river itself, which is about 200 yards away. The standard fee is EC$20.00 per person.

After about three quarters of a mile, the river narrows and the way is stopped by miniature rapids. Here you can get out and explore the surrounding secondary forest, before joining your boat once more for the return trip.

Portsmouth

Portsmouth is a popular call for yachts and a centre for Caribbean inter-island trading ships. Traditional sloops and schooners are still built along the shore. It is different from Roseau. This is very much a seaport town of schooner hands, captains of tramp steamers, hucksters and street-wise youth, and therefore has a jaunty, buccaneering air about it. The original British colonists planned it as the capital of the island, but commerce and government remained firmly concentrated in Roseau. This neglect and lack of activity over

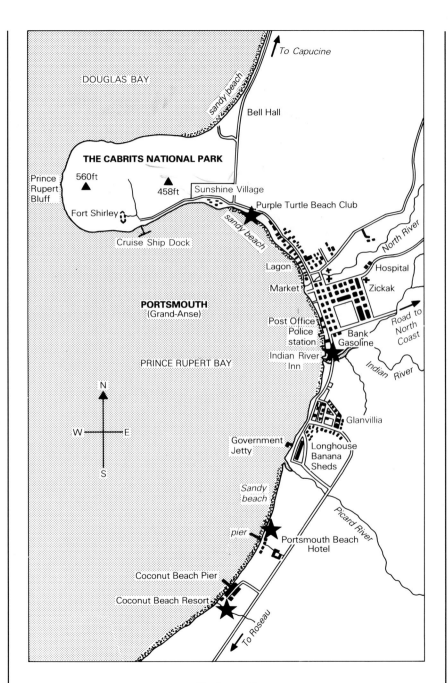

Portsmouth

the years has created a 'North versus South, Roseau versus Portsmouth' attitude to district affairs, which is most marked in political matters, and is always a subject of contention at election time.

The visitor can obtain a number of services at Portsmouth. Immigration and customs are situated at the Police Station on Bay Street. The banks, gas station and Tourist Board agency are all within 100 yards of the landing jetty. Up the hill from the Roman Catholic Church is the Portsmouth Hospital.

Small guest houses with basic facilities are located in Portsmouth. Bars and restaurants serve simple snacks and local dishes. Hotels along Picard Beach provide resort-type accommodation. The nearest refreshment stops to the Cabrits National Park are the Purple Turtle Beach Club, the Umbrella Bar at Sunshine Village Resort and Prince Rupert's Tavern in the park itself.

The market, near the end of Bay Street, offers local fruit and vegetables early on Saturday mornings, shops stock a good variety of groceries and Waldron's bakery on Rodney Street is recommended for bread and cakes. As already mentioned, boat tours up the Indian River can be arranged with guides near the jetty at Boroughs Square.

| 12 |
The Carib Territory

The mixed descendants of the last Island Caribs who inhabited the Lesser Antilles live on the north-east coast of Dominica. This simple fact has been so exaggerated and distorted over the last thirty years of tourism publicity, that there tends to be much misunderstanding, bewilderment and eventual disappointment among visitors who come to view the Carib Territory as one of the 'attractions' of Dominica.

Some years ago, before the motorable road went completely through this area, I was travelling with a group of visitors who had rocked and jolted across the island to see the 'Indian Reservation' as they called it. Having passed through all the scattered hamlets which made up the isolated community, the vehicle reached the end of the road and turned around to go back to Roseau. Immediately there was the plaintive wail of North American accents from the

Carib children at Sineku

rear of the Land Rover 'But where's the Carib Village?'

It struck me at once what the problem was. Somewhere, in all the glossy promotional hype, they had been led to believe that here they would see a primitive tribe in its last halcyon days; with thatched huts, grass skirts, a chief in feathers and perhaps a few hula-hula dancers. It is nothing like that at all.

Visually there is little to differentiate it from any other part of rural Dominica. The same small farms of mixed crops dominated by bananas and coconuts are clustered around the roadside and surrounding hills. The same houses, some of concrete, some of wood surrounded by tidy flower gardens face onto the road. One slight distinction may be that some of the wooden houses are raised on stilts to shelter drying timber, cocoa, coffee or reeds for basket making. Increasingly you'll see the family pick-up truck parked nearby and television aerials sprouting from bamboo poles. Perhaps a thatched outhouse or kitchen utilising traditional materials and building methods may be seen.

Only three things hint that here live the remnants of a disappearing

**A Carib canoe-builder at Salybia inspects his finished product
while his Creole wife and child look on**

tribe: the small craft shops selling the basketwork which follows styles and patterns handed down for centuries; now and then the sight of a half-finished canoe being hollowed out of the single trunk of a giant *Gommier* tree and the sight of people whose skin tone and facial structure vaguely recall the Mongolian origin of their forefathers, who once had free rein over all these islands.

The weakening of their hold on Dominica began from the time that the first Spanish caravelles dropped anchor in Prince Rupert's Bay, shortly after the second voyage of Columbus. From then on, ships of all nations came regularly to collect wood and water and to trade with the Caribs for fruit and cassava flour. For almost two centuries, contact was limited to trading and occasional skirmishes, but by the mid seventeenth century Dominica had become a refuge for Caribs retreating from the other islands where the surge of French, English and Dutch colonisation was sweeping them off their ancestral lands. The rugged mountains, thick forests and iron coastline provided a natural citadel for the final retreat. From this base they made attacks on the fledgling European colonies and suffered at least two massacres in retaliation; one at Anse De Mai in 1635 and another in 1674 at the village which is still called Massacre today.

Religion was used as the first tool of subjugation and missionaries of the Dominican, Capucine and Jesuit Orders installed themselves at various points on the island. They had little spiritual success but collected masses of anthropological data on the Carib language and way of life. At the same time propaganda was being used to justify extermination. Pamphleteers in Europe were having a field day on the subject of Carib cannibalism, outdoing each other to create ever more gory accounts about the consumption of human flesh. One of them, Rochefort, has Carib gourmets comparing the taste and texture of various European nationalities. Being a Frenchman, his story concludes of course, that the French were the most tasty! It appears, however, from the more balanced accounts of respected missionaries that such tales of cannibalism were greatly exaggerated and may have been based on the occasional ceremonial use of ancestor and enemy remains.

By 1700 French lumbermen had established their ateliers along the leeward coast and soon the Caribs were withdrawing to the windward side, exchanging land rights for rum, brass bowls, iron axes, cutlasses and hoes.

When the British formally took over in 1763 European conquest was complete. British surveyors divided the island up into lots for sale and plantations were established around the island. Only 232 acres of mountainous land and rocky shoreline at Salybia were left for the Caribs. This was done, legend has it, at the request of Queen Charlotte, wife of George III. This subsequently developed into the myth that Charlotte had left them half of Dominica – a myth which today many older Caribs consider, erroneously, to be an historical fact.

For another 130 years the Caribs were left to themselves, shadowy figures hardly seen by the growing Creole society of African slaves, free men and European officials and landowners. Now and then they appeared in the estate yards and at Sunday markets to sell baskets and fish, but quickly dissolved into the mountains once more along forest tracks towards Salybia.

When Sir Robert Hamilton was sent out by the British Colonial Office as Commissioner in 1893 to find out why Dominica was: *more backward and less developed than almost any other of the islands*, and why its people were: *less prosperous and contented than Her Majesty's other West Indian subjects*, he received a tragic little letter from the Caribs:

In the name of God. My Lord, We humble beg of your kindness to accept our petition of your poor people, Indians or Caraibe, of Salibia, to . . . emplore the marcy of our Beloved Mother and Queen Victoria, for her poor and unfortunate childrens. We dont have nothings to support us, no church, no school, no shope, no store. We are very far in the forest; no money, no dress . . . They call us wild savages. No my beloved Queen, it is not savages but poverty. We humble kneel down in your feet to beg of your assistance. Accept your humble childrens of Salibia . . .

Nine years afterwards an enlightened Administrator, Hesketh Bell, sent a lengthy report to the Colonial Office making certain proposals for the future of the Caribs. He advised that 3,700 acres should be set aside for them and that a chief should be officially recognised by the colony and given a token allowance of £6 annually. This was approved, and a year later the chief was invested with a silver-headed staff and ceremonial sash.

Economically and socially, however, there was no improvement and emotions flared up in September 1930 in a conflict with police over smuggling. It was only in 1970 that a motorable road was cut through the area and telephones and electricity followed in the 1980s. Bananas and coconuts have improved earnings, but because all the land is owned in common, it is intensively used and therefore has the most serious soil erosion problem on Dominica and has lost many of its smaller streams through deforestation.

The position of the Chief is less romantic than most visitors like to believe. In 1952 a Carib Council was created as part of a local government system for the whole island. Legislation was upgraded at Independence in 1978 with the Carib Reserve Act. There are elections every five years and the chairman of the council is designated the 'Chief'. Except for this title, he plays the same role as all the other Village Council chairmen in Dominica. To further confuse the matter, the Carib Territory, as it is now popularly called, also has a Parliamentary Representative who sits in the House of Assembly in Roseau and is elected every five years. The Chief and the Parliamentary Representative usually make an effort to relate to one another, but in fact the Representative sitting in the nation's House of Assembly has more power than the Chief. However, the Chief is more in demand as the spokesman for the Territory,

The Salibisie Islets off the bay at Salibya

particularly by visiting journalists and international conferences on Amerindian and Aboriginal affairs.

It is a sad irony that this tribe of seafarers, after whom the waters of the Caribbean have been named, should end up in a corner of the island where access to the sea is almost impossible. There are only two difficult landing places on this wild and dramatic shoreline. One is at Salybia Bay where you can see the rocky Salibisie Islets and the Church of St Marie with its altar carved in the shape of a canoe.

Walking straight down the hill opposite the Salybia Police Station you come to the mouth of the Crayfish or Isulukati River where waterfalls cascade from rock pools over a stony ledge into the sea. A fifteen minute walk from the hamlet of Sineku takes you to **L'escalier Tete Chien** or the Snake's Staircase – Tête Chien being the local name for the boa constrictor because its head looks like that of a dog. Geologically, this rock formation is called a dyke. It resembles a gigantic petrified serpent crawling up the hillside from the ocean with its back crystalised into wedges of rock which forms a natural staircase. This 'escalier' features prominently in Carib myth and folklore.

Natural landmarks such as the rock at Sineku are highlights of ancient Carib mythology. A huge rock overlooking Pagua River near Atkinson, the islets off Londonderry beach, a cave near Kraibo Bay at Wesley were once featured in Carib tales, most of which have long been forgotten.

The strongest link with the past however are the Carib baskets which are sold in little craft shops all along the road through the Carib Territory. The brown, white and black designs of the larouma reed have been handed down from generation to generation. The square paniers and side bags are made in two layers with heliconia leaves in between. This waterproof design is a remnant from the days when food and goods had to be kept dry from sea spray in the open canoes and from rainfall along the forest trails across the mountainous interior. Such a basket is the most authentic souvenir you can get of the Caribbean and of the people who gave the region its name.

| 13 |
The South Coast

Because there is no road around the extreme southern end of the island a visit to the south and southwest shoreline must be made via two separate routes. Both of these branch off from the village of **Loubiere**. One road follows the coast southwards through Pointe Michel and Soufriere to Scotts Head or **Cashacrou**. The other cuts across the southern mountains past Bellevue Chopin and Pichelin to Geneva, then a fork in the road gives you the choice of going either to **Grand Bay** or **Petite Savanne** where the road is once again stopped by steep mountains.

Cashacrou route

First we shall head for Cashacrou driving beneath the sheer cliffs called Solomon. Here on 7 September, 1778 the French fought back the British time and time again as they made their way from Pointe Michel to capture Roseau. Pointe Michel was a centre for French coffee planters 200 years ago and also received an influx of refugees from Martinique escaping the eruption of Mont Pele in 1902.

Further on, the road winds inland, rising behind the peak of La Sorcier from the top of which, legend has it, Carib men threw their unfaithful wives. We can now look down into Soufriere Bay with Cashacrou at its southern end. Sites to visit in **Soufriere** are the ruins of the old sugar and lime factory and the Catholic church with its vibrant mural depicting village life. In the valley behind the village are the sulphur springs which give the area its name. These are reached by driving along the road up the valley past the village school and then less than half a mile further on, turning left. When the French held Dominica, they built baths here for their soldiers. The area is like a small walk-in volcano and is more dramatic than the springs at Wotton Waven. Energetic hikers can scale the narrow track which leads up the mountains to Tete Morne and over to Grand Bay. Hot springs are also active in the water along the seashore between Soufriere and Scotts Head, and on the sea bed in front of the Church.

Scott's head or Cashacrou Point and Soufriere Bay are dominated by the summit of La Sorcier in the foreground

The ruins of **Fort Cashacrou** remain on the headland which you reach along the narrow isthmus. Most of the batteries and ramparts of the fort have fallen over the cliffs into the sea, but it was an important defence post, involved in military action between the British and French in 1778 and 1805. Looking back eastward you see the Atlantic swells crashing on the right and the placid Caribbean lapping gently on the left. Cashacrou is the original Carib name which means 'that which is being eaten' (by the sea). The English called it Scotts Head after Captain Scott, one of those who, along with Douglas and Rollo, gave their names to places in Dominica after capturing the island from the French in 1761. Do not believe people who tell you that it was named after a Scotsman who had his head chopped off there! Snorkelling and Scuba diving around the point are spectacular. Beautiful coral reefs have grown upon the submerged outcrops of volcanic rock. Above water, on a clear day you get a wonderful view north across the bay and along the coast as far as Grand Savannah. Looking south you see the blue green pyramid of Martinique and Mont Pele on the horizon.

Grand Bay and Petite Savanne

The road from Loubiere to Grand Bay is a dramatic route of precipices and panoramas with lush green ravines on one hand and hanging foliage on the other. In Pichelin you may notice vertiver grass laid out to dry on the road. Driving over it does no harm. In fact it helps loosen the stalks which are plaited into cord to make the famous Dominican straw mats.

The main point of interest in Grand Bay is the Church with local paintings over the doors. The belfry was moved up onto the hilltop so that its sound could be heard over a wider area. On a rainy day water gushes through the mouths of gargoyles perched along the roof of the church. Overlooking the cemetery is the oldest crucifix on the island carved from solid stone in about 1720. The long steep main street through the village of Grand Bay is called L'allay. At the top of it you can continue up the hill to Tete Morne from where

The villages of Loubiere and Pointe Michel on either side of the Solomon Cliffs, south of Roseau

there are spectacular views across Grand Bay and along the Soufriere Valley to the Caribbean Sea. A zig-zag track leads down a thousand feet from here to Soufriere.

Back on the road towards Petite Savanne you pass the ruined Geneva sugar mill. This estate is associated with the childhood of the Dominican novelist Jean Rhys and is the setting for part of her novel *Wide Sargasso Sea*.

The sea lashes at the road beneath the cliffs of Dubuc and you get wonderful views westward across the bay. There are other old sugar mills at Stowe and Bagatelle near the quaint fishing village of Fond St Jean. Turning towards the hills once more we make for Petite Savanne, a village of the descendants of the first French settlers. Petite Savanne is a centre of the bay-oil industry and you may pass several sweet-scented distilleries at work. It also boasts the most dramatic cricket field in the West Indies where two sides of the boundary line run along a cliff edge which drops into the surging Atlantic. Hit six runs and your ball is afloat in the Martinique channel!

The motorable road ends at Petite Savanne but hikers may wish to continue on foot along the track which climbs up Morne Paix Bouche and over to Pointe Mulatre. From the highest point you can see steam rising from the Boiling Lake and Valley of Desolation across the mountains.

| 14 |
The East Coast

The early French settlers called it *Au Vent*, and it is still known by that name in our local Creole. To the English, it was 'Windward Side', and today it is generally referred to as 'the South-East'. But whichever name we use, it is a rugged, windswept shoreline of dark, deserted beaches and iron cliffs, lashed by waves all the way from Africa. The landscape is defiant. The volcanic bluffs jut out like guardian lions, the foliage like windblown manes swept back by the constant force of the easterly trade winds.

This coast is divided by the motorable road into two sections. The first runs from **Castle Bruce** to **Petite Soufriere**. The other runs from **Rosalie** to La Riviere Blanche at **Point Mulatre**. The junction of these two routes is near the large government quarry known as 'Tarrish Pit' just over two miles east of Pont Casse.

Castle Bruce to Petite Soufriere

This first route takes you past the entrance to the Emerald Pool at the northern-most section of the Trois Pitons National Park. You drive down through the Belle Fille Valley to the broad river plain of Castle Bruce Estate. The final mile and a half is one of the longest sections of straight road on the island. Castle Bruce Estate is now divided up into numerous small farms, as a result of a conflict between workers' representatives and the estate management in 1972. In the eighteenth century it was owned by Captain James Bruce, military engineer, who gave the estate his name and planted it in sugar cane.

Beautiful St David Bay or Anse Quanary, is very similar to Pagua Bay further north, and is just as dangerous. Its distinctive feature is the couple of forested islets off the southern point of the bay. In spite of the heavy swell and powerful waves, fishermen go out into the Atlantic from this bay, and you will always see several Carib canoes drawn up underneath the palms. Because of the forceful undertow, which has resulted in several drownings over the years, swimming in the ocean here is not advised. However, a large fresh-water lagoon at the mouth of the river provides safer swimming within sight and sound of the breakers.

Continuing on the road to Petite Soufriere, one gets spectacular views to the north and south along the coast, as you pass through hamlets such as Tranto, Morpo and Good Hope, before reaching Saint Sauveur. This village lies in the bay of Grand Marigot, pronounced in the French fashion, unlike Marigot village in the north, whose pronunciation has been Anglicised with heavy emphasis on the 't' at the end of the word. On this part of the coast too, the processing of bay leaves is an important industry and you may see one or two small distilleries in operation. The quaint village church is the main architectural feature of this village.

You climb again to cross the ridge towards Petite Soufriere, a village of scattered houses perched here and there upon steep slopes, which sweep down to the rocky shore. Although its name alludes to small sulphur springs, there is no evidence of these and there is no record of any having existed in the area, so the origin of the name is something of a mystery. The motorable road ends here, but walkers can take a short hike along the old trace dating from the eighteenth century, which rises and falls around a couple of headlands towards Rosalie. This walk will give you an idea of what visiting this entire coast was like, before motorable roads were cut along it in the 1960s.

Rosalie to Pointe Mulatre

To visit the south east coast you start again from the Tarrish Pit junction, driving through extensive banana and citrus cultivations until you reach Rosalie. Like all streams which still flow from the forest and then continue through large, undivided plantations, Rosalie River is one of the better preserved waterways on Dominica. Exploring up the banks will reveal a beautiful assortment of large river pools. At Rosalie you see the old aquaduct arch, one of the last on the island, which carried water to the sugar mill.

Rosalie Estate was originally owned by a syndicate of eighteenth century British Governors of the island and features prominently in the Afro-Caribbean Maroon conflicts. It was the site of the Maroon raid in 1786, led by Chief Balla. Near the shore, a deserted and ruined church, looking like a transplant from Normandy, bears testimony to the village which once existed there. The ruins of an old crane platform on Rosalie Point is a relic of the days when ships went around the island to collect sugar, limes, coffee and cocoa from the isolated estates. Here again, this windswept beach, with its expanse of volcanic boulders and black sand, is very dangerous for swimming.

Turning once more onto the main road, you cross the low concrete bridge heading south. You can turn right into the hills to the mountain village of Grand Fond. It is situated along the old 'Chemin L'Etang' or Lake Road, which was once the most important footpath across the island before the advent of the motorable road.

Heading southwards, however, you climb through the villages of Riviere Cyrique and Morne Jaune, before diving down towards La Plaine. For such a mountainous coast, this is indeed an unexpected expanse of open country. It is really a fan-shaped, rocky outflow from the ancient volcanoes of the Grand Soufriere hills, and it ends in a long, precipitous, high cliff dropping off into the sea. The early French settlers called it simply, La Plaine, and they must have enjoyed living there, judging by the estate names such as Felicité, Plaisance and Cote D'Or. Before entering La Plaine proper, you pass Bout Sable Bay, another stretch of black sand, towering cliffs and dangerous seas. One intrepid bather, US millionaire

Bout Sable Bay on the East Coast near La Plaine.
On the horizon is Rosalie Point with Petite Soufriere behind.

John D Archbold, and his wife, Ann, almost lost their lives here in the 1940s, but were saved by brave villagers, who pulled them ashore through the thundering surf. In gratitude, Mr Archbold gave the village its first health clinic. The incident was witnessed by British author Alec Waugh and forms part of his book *The Sugar Islands*.

At Case O'Gowerie, there is a memorial to villagers who died during an uprising against the imposition of Land Tax in 1893. A British warship, *HMS Mohawk*, was sent to La Plaine, and police and marines were landed to confront the demonstrators. High up the valley behind the village is the Sari-Sari waterfall.

From La Plaine, we continue through La Ronde, La Fanchette and Boetica, along a road which was the engineering achievement of its day. Five men lost their lives in the construction of a massive causeway across the deep Boetica Gorge.

At Delices, we are once more in bay leaf country, although bananas have increasingly taken over in recent years. Moving through the village past La Roche, you get to Pointe Mulatre Bay, and the mouth of La Riviere Blanche or White River, whose source is the Boiling Lake. Its milky-white look is quite healthy, for the

Bathers enjoy wading in the rapids of Riviere Blanche, the White River, at Pointe Mulatre. The source of this milky, mineral-rich water is the Boiling Lake

water is composed of sulphurous minerals which many bathers believe have recuperative qualities. On the way through La Roche you get a glimpse of the Victoria Falls about a mile further up the valley.

Across the river is Pointe Mulatre Estate, once a flourishing sugar and coffee plantation, with an old French graveyard and several ruins. In the 1950s a scheme by a Swedish businessman to turn Pointe Mulatre into a Scandinavian retirement colony collapsed, and some of the deserted holiday homes still stand in the bush. Here the motorable road ends, but hikers can continue on foot along the old trace over Morne Paix Bouche ('Hush-Your-Mouth' because it is such steep walking), and down the other side into Petite Savanne, where a motorable road begins again along the south coast towards Roseau.

Coral sand and shady palms at Woodford Bay *(overleaf)*

| 15 |
The North Coast

The north and north-eastern coastline, running from Pagua Bay to Capucine Point, can be divided into three sections. The first, from **Pagua** to **Crompton Point**, faces more directly into the rough Atlantic swells and the shoreline is broken into sharp cliffs and unprotected coves and beaches. The second section is quite different as the coast makes an abrupt turn at Crompton Point. From there until you reach **Anse Soldat**, it is lined with sandy coves of varying sizes, protected by low, windswept headlands pointing towards the flat French coral island of Marie-galante. The third section is from Anse Soldat to **Pennville**. At Blenheim, the coastline suddenly changes direction and character once more. Spectacular precipices soar above the ocean, villages are perched on cliff-tops and each stream cuts its way through a deep abyss, tumbling over waterfalls into the sea. Except at Thibaud, there are no beaches. It is the visual impact of this section of the north coast which is its greatest attraction.

You may approach the north coast from either end. Driving from Portsmouth, you cut across what I call 'the Neck' of Dominica, and arrive on the coast at Blenheim. From there you have a choice of turning north to Vieille Case and Pennville, or continuing eastward along the coast to Pagua. If you are coming from the other direction, either from the Transinsular Road or the Carib Territory, you arrive at Pagua.

Pagua to Crompton Point

The first village you meet after Pagua Bay is **Marigot**. The people of Marigot and **Wesley**, which is situated further along the coast after Londonderry Beach, have a rather different history from other Dominicans. During the last half of the nineteenth century, a British company of chocolate manufacturers decided to buy the old, derelict estates in that area for cocoa production. The independent Dominican peasantry which had grown up after emancipation had no desire to revert to being estate labourers. The company therefore turned to Antigua and certain other Leeward Islands for its labour force. As a result, we find that the villagers of Marigot and Wesley speak no French Creole, have no traditional French-influenced folklore, and that the vast majority are Methodists and Evangelical Fundamentalists rather than Roman Catholics. Even the name of the old French Catholic parish of La Soye has been changed to *Wesley* after the founder of Methodism.

Between Wesley and Marigot is Dominica's first airport: **Melville Hall**. It was originally planned in 1944, but had to await the completion of a road to Roseau in 1956 before construction could proceed. It was completed in 1958 and was the island's only airport until **Canefield** was opened in 1981. Woodford Hill is the area earmarked by planners for a still larger airport, capable of taking jet aircraft.

Crompton Point to Anse Soldat

It is along this stretch of coast that you find most of the best beaches on Dominica. The sand varies from jet black at L'Ance Noir to golden, powdered coral at Woodford Bay and Pointe Baptiste. Most of the beaches are sheltered by rocky islets and coral reefs. This makes arrival by sea dangerous, although about five of these bays

Glistening black sand on the dramatic but dangerous Londonderry Beach

are used by small fishing boats, whose captains are skilled in dodging the reefs and outcrops of volcanic rock which dot their entrances.

At **Woodford Bay** there is a lovely stretch of golden sand beach with sheltered swimming, protected by coral reefs. In 1948 the 'discovery scene' in a British film about Christopher Columbus was filmed here. The best beaches for bathing along this coast are Woodford Bay, L'Ance Tortue or Turtle Bay, Pointe Baptiste and Hampstead Beach. I would put Hodges Beach, Anse De Mai and Anse Soldat in a second category. There are others, such as Eden, Anse Noir and Hampstead River Bay, which are attractive, but not ideal for swimming.

One problem for visitors using the older official Government maps of Dominica, is that the north coast has been badly researched. Anse De Mai is printed in the wrong place, and several other bays and points are not named. You may therefore not find some of the bays mentioned above printed on the official maps.

The motorable road does not get down to most of these beaches, and you may have to walk to reach some of them. Others are served by rugged estate roads which are in bad repair and ordinary vehicles could get stuck during rainy periods. All beaches in Dominica are public up to high water mark (i.e., where the sand ends and vegetation begins). Although the majority of paths are 'public rights-of-way' by tradition rather than by law, you must respect the rights of owners through whose land you may have to pass to reach the beach.

Calibishie is perhaps the most pleasant village along this coast. It is noted for the colourful hedges along the roadside and its neat houses and gardens. It is also the only part of Dominica sheltered by a continuous barrier reef, over a mile long. The sheltered lagoon inside the reef and the thin line of golden sand beneath the palm trees is reminiscent of a Pacific island village, rather than the Caribbean. At Calibishie, you can refresh yourself at the Almond Tree restaurant along the seashore in the centre of the village.

Near Calibishie is **Pointe Baptiste**, a beautiful private nature reserve which includes coastal forest, black and white sand beaches and a headland of red rock sculptured by the wind, rain and sea. The traditional-style wooden family home, now a guest house, looks over a panoramic seascape fringed by mountains, bays, points and islands. In earlier days, the Napier family, who lived there, played host at various times to personalities such as W. Somerset Maugham,

Sunset over Calibishie Bay

Noel Coward, Jean Rhys, Alec Waugh, Princess Margaret and the US presidential candidate Adali Stevenson.

In the sea off Calibishie there are two rocky islets known collectively as Porte La Fin, the Gate of Hell. They were once joined by a natural archway which collapsed in 1954, but the impression of a rugged archway to the underworld is still very clear.

At the picturesque fishing port of **Anse De Mai**, it is possible to make arrangements for a day trip in an open fishing boat to the neighbouring French island of Marie-galante. This village was the site of a massacre of Caribs led by a French Captain Du Mé in 1635. Today it is spelt De Mai. Hampstead and Blenheim are both large coconut estates and near the roadside you may see copra being produced on the site of the old sugar and lime factories. The old works at Hampstead has the best preserved water wheel in Dominica.

Anse Soldat to Pennville

There is a junction in the road at Blenheim Estate, and here you turn northwards towards **Vieille Case** and **Pennville**. This roller-coaster road was originally cut by pick-axe and shovel along the edge of spurs and precipices, and therefore has some of the tightest hair-pin bends and steepest inclines of any road on the island. It also has the most spectacular views. The north coast is spread out like extended fingers beneath you. Green, forested knuckles slope towards rocky red fingertips splashed with foam. At Vieille Case you can descend to the dare-devil landing place of Au Tou, where fishermen race the giant breakers to haul their boats up onto a ramp of volcanic rock. At Pennville you almost look down onto the neighbouring French islands of Les Saintes. Here you would have had a ringside seat at the Battle of the Saints, the most important sea battle in the Caribbean, fought between the British, under Admiral Rodney, and the French, under Compte De Grasse, on 12 April 1782.

Both villages of Pennville and Vieille Case have strong French links. They were originally settled by French peasant farmers from Guadeloupe and Marie-galante in the early eighteenth century, and their close proximity to these islands is still an important factor in village life. Many villagers live and work in Marie-galante, and the use of French Creole is stronger than in many other villages. The first Christian mass was celebrated here by French missionaries in

The Vieille Case village church rises out of lush vegetation on the slopes of Morne aux Diable

1646, and the heavy stone Vieille Case church is interesting for its rather Hispanic facade, unusual in Dominica, and for its colourful murals.

From Pennville, there is a tortuous but beautiful track which climbs up and down the extreme north of the island to reach Capucine, where the motorable road begins again. Work is slowly progressing to cut a motorable road across the mountains from Pennville to Douglas Bay, but until this is completed, motorists will have to return by the route they came on, savouring the views of the north coast as they drive back.

| 16 |
The West Coast

The entire west coast of Dominica, from **Cashacrou** in the south to **Capucine** in the north, lies in the rain shadow zone and therefore tends to be hotter than other parts of the island, and has dry scrubland vegetation. On some cliffs you will find numerous species of cactus, and for this reason one of the villages on the coast is called Morne Rachette. The soil, up to one or two miles inland, is very shallow and cannot support the verdant forests which grow at higher elevations. It is a very rocky coastline, with cliffs and valleys alternating all along the shore.

While travelling past sections where the road has been cut into the hillside, you will notice different lines of strata. These are layers of volcanic ash and debris deposited on top of one another over thousands of years. In some areas, there is evidence of coral limestone, worn boulders and ancient sea shells, at places over one hundred feet above sea level. This is because, millions of years ago, the island was tilted sideways and the entire west coast was submerged below the surface of the Caribbean Sea.

The beaches along this coast are all of grey, volcanic sand. The best of them are at Mero, Batalie, Prince Rupert's Bay, Douglas Bay and Toucari. The water is usually very calm, sheltered as it is by the hills and protected by the island itself from the Atlantic swells. Further out to sea, this can, however, make sailing and wind surfing difficult. Sudden calms are followed by abrupt down-draughts of wind, which rush through the valleys, and bounce off the hillsides as the easterly Trade Winds cross the mountainous interior. This is what usually makes landing at Canefield Airport such a bouncy affair.

Driving north from Roseau, one enters Canefield Estate, once one of the largest sugar and lime plantations in Dominica. The old sugar and lime works have been converted into the **Old Mill Cultural Centre** which is described in Chapter 18. The lime and sugar fields are now covered with industrial sheds, suburban houses and the Canefield Airport.

At the airport there is a junction which turns up onto the Imperial

The Old Mill Cultural Centre and Museum at Canefield, a remnant of the
days when sugar, coffee and limes were Dominica's main crops

Road on the way to Pont Cassé. This road, completed in about
1906, was built with a grant of funds from the British Treasury and
was given the incongruous title *The Imperial Road*. A scheme to
bring out British settlers to live along the road failed, but the name
remains. It zig-zags up the hill in a series of hair-pin bends through
Canefield, Roger and along the Antrim Valley past Springfield, Mount
Joy, L'Imprevue and Sylvania to the roundabout at Pont Cassé. It
is seven miles shorter than going around via Layou.

Continuing along the west coast, we pass through **Massacre**,
named after a massacre of Caribs by the English in 1674. The story
surrounding this event is quite a saga, involving the half-caste Carib
Chief, *Carib Warner*, killed by his English half-brother Phillip, for
trying to keep Dominica as a bastion for the Caribs of the Lesser
Antilles. After passing through the crowded clutter of Mahaut, we
come to Belfast, the site of Dominica Coconut Products' factory,
one of our success stories. Here, coconut copra, from farms all over
the island, is turned into oil, soap, detergent and cosmetics. Rum
is also produced from sugar cane in the old Belfast estate distillery.
One mile further on is Rodney's Rock, named after the British
Admiral. All sorts of stories surround this black lava headland,

suggesting its involvement with Rodney as he pursued the French to the Battle of the Saints. I have, however, never found any proof that, other than being given his name, it played any part in the action of April 1782.

After passing beneath Tarreau Cliffs, we enter the **Layou** Valley. The river is the largest and longest in Dominica, absorbing water from the widest watershed area in the interior. The road which leads up the valley to Pont Cassé passes by the Hillsborough plant propagation station, the Layou River Hotel, York Valley, Layou Park, the junction to Warner Village and Layou Valley Inn, before reaching the Pont Cassé roundabout. There are several beautiful river pools worth exploring. The Layou River Hotel has a natural pool of its own, but there is an even better one upstream from the York Valley bridge. Here, a warm water spring has been dammed on the river bank so that you can jump from warm water into cold. At Cassada Gardens, about a mile further on, you turn left off the main road towards another large pool above which hangs a narrow 'swing bridge', suspended across the gorge. A real adventure is to spend the day going down the Layou Gorge, starting in the middle of the island at Bells. It is only recommended for the fit and agile, as the rocks and rapids are treacherous.

Back on the coast, crossing the Layou Bridge, we pass Hillsborough Estate, once a thriving tobacco plantation, now also growing coconuts, cocoa and coffee. Perhaps you may see cocoa lying out to dry among the ruins of the large old factory yard. Above is the estate house with a birds-eye view of the whole valley. This estate was the source of our Hillsborough cigars and cigarettes, now made with imported tobacco because, like so much else, it is cheaper to import than to produce locally. Hillsborough is also the setting for several slave novels, and St Joseph Village, further north, was used as a location in the US horror movie *The Seventh Sign*, filmed in 1987.

Next, we come to Castaways Hotel. Opened in 1961, it was the first of its kind, in that it was constructed specifically as an hotel. Its large, balconied rooms all look over the long stretch of Mero beach. Driving on, we come to Macoucherie Estate, which has one of the two rum distilleries on the island. It is also one of the last cane mills in the West Indies powered by water. During crop time the colourful bustle of activity takes us back through the centuries to the time when sugar was king.

We are now entering the dryest part of Dominica, as we pass the village of Salisbury and cross the Grand Savannah. Batalie Estate was once owned by the energetic Dr John Imray, over a hundred years ago. Here, he carried out his agricultural experiments to find new crops for the island after the collapse of sugar. It was here that he first introduced limes, which brought great prosperity to Dominica. You can enjoy a swim at Batalie beach or in the river mouth.

From here, we pass the villages of Coulibistrie, Colihaut, Bioche and Dublanc, each tucked into narrow valleys between high cliffs. Until 1969 they were more easily reached by sea than by road. Colihaut's claim to fame is that it was the centre for rebellious Republican Frenchmen during the French Revolution two hundred years ago. They conspired with the Maroons in the mountains in the hope that they would topple the British and take over the island for the new Republic. Colihaut must have been quite a place in its day, for in 1828 it boasted twelve billiard tables and sixteen taverns!

Just after leaving Dublanc, you can turn right onto the agricultural feeder road to Syndicate at the foot of **Morne Diablotin**. Walking into the forest from the end of the road you may be lucky enough to see parrots, particularly in the very early morning and at dusk. There is a track to a point known as the 'parrot perch' where, from the top of a cliff, you get a view across the forest canopy and the parrots are best observed. Syndicate is also the start for the hike to the top of Morne Diablotin. Remember that even at the end of this motorable road you still have almost 3000 feet to climb on foot with frequent pull-ups, using your hands as well. It is, however, the best place to experience the rain forest in its finest form. Syndicate adjoins **Morne Plaisance**, another fine rain forest area, which can be reached via the Dominica Timbers road from 'Ti Baye near Picard.

The last main feature on our drive up the west coast is **Morne Espagnol**, named for the early Spanish sailors who called regularly at Prince Rupert's Bay. The English called it Barbers Block, because its shape resembled the rounded wooden block on which barbers made wigs in the eighteenth century. Today, the mountain top bristles with telecommunications aerials and dishes, part of Dominica's modern TV and telephone systems.

The final section of the coast has already been described in the chapter on the Cabrits National Park. Beyond the Cabrits, you drive to the northernmost tip at Capucine, passing the settlements of Tan-Tan, Savanne Paille, picturesque Toucari; Cottage and Clifton on the way.

| 17 |
Underwater adventures

The beauty of Dominica is as spectacular below the surface of the sea as it is above. Coral reefs growing atop craggy outcrops of submerged volcanic rock formations add a new element to the adventure of scuba diving in the Caribbean.

Diving is a relatively new sport on Dominica. The sites are virtually unexplored and every so often new locations are discovered around the coast. One of the pioneers of scuba diving here is Derek Perryman, a former airline pilot, as adventurous underwater as he is in the air. He operates **Dive Dominica**, with its dive shop situated at Castle Comfort Guest House just south of Roseau. Derek has introduced some of the biggest names in scuba diving to the marvels of Dominica's underwater world. Recent coverage in diving magazines has given Dominica some exciting write-ups, describing thrilling dive sites of international quality – and marveling at the 'windowpane' visibility. Dramatic drop-offs, wall dives, wrecks, caves, canyons, arches and pinnacles offer adventure to both the novice and experienced diver.

Around Scotts Head, beautiful reefs of staghorn and brain coral drop suddenly off into the deep blue waters of a volcanically formed abyss. Across the bay at L'Abym a sheer cliff along the face of an eroded volcanic cone slices down into the sea and continues for hundreds of feet below the surface providing a stunning wall dive.

Elsewhere in the bay, divers swim through gurgling bubbles created by air rising from volcanic fissures on the sea bed. As one travel writer put it 'here the sea sings' and gives one the feeling of swimming through champagne.

On the north side of the Cabrits, coral grows around huge submerged boulders. Across this marine park at Douglas Bay a section of the cliff has fallen into the sea at the end of Douglas Point;

Scuba diver (DIVE DOMINICA) *(opposite)*

Reef fish at Cashacrou (DIVE DOMINICA) *(overleaf)*

in falling it cracked again thus creating a long narrow crevice to be explored by intrepid divers. These are just some of the underwater adventures which a growing number of scuba divers are discovering around our island.

The main sites are in the south-west of the island, particularly around **Scotts Head** and **Soufriere Bay**, but locations at the other end of the island in the north-west near Toucari and Capucine are also tempting and include wrecks of an iron-hulled sailing ship and a World War I gunboat. The dive shop's 33 ft and 24 ft dive boats get divers to most sites within 20 minutes. Dive Dominica offers the most comprehensive facilities available, including night dives, dive packages, resort courses, certification courses, hotel/dive packages, snorkeling, equipment rentals, repair and sales, air fills and boat charters. This professionally run dive resort is approved by the US National Association of Underwater Instructors (NAUI). Anchorage Hotel, next door to Dive Dominica, and the Portsmouth Beach Hotel, also offer scuba diving facilities with two 30 ft speed boats, equipment rentals, special packages and courses, also backed by the approval of NAUI. Another scuba diving outfit offering all services operates out of Castaways Hotel at Mero.

| 18 |
Handicrafts

Carib handicrafts are unique because the designs have been handed down from one generation to the next, since long before the time of Columbus. The designs originated in the rainforests of the Orinoco River Basin. Today similar designs using the same materials as those of the Island Caribs are still made by the Amerindian tribes along the banks of the Orinoco. This is fascinating considering that there has been no interaction for over five hundred years and yet the material and styles survive independently. This makes the possession of a Carib basket more than just the souvenir of a visit but gives a tangible link with the Caribbean before 1492.

Today, we think of handicrafts as decorative pieces of local work made merely for sale to tourists and for adorning the walls and floors of houses. This is a relatively recent viewpoint since most of our local handicrafts originated as vital pieces of equipment for domestic use.

Carib baskets were the only form of baggage containers for most of the people. The Cassava coulevre and sifter were important processing tools. Grass hats and mats were the only such things available before imported items flooded the market with foreign alternatives. Today, bamboo, coconut and tree fern or fwigé are being used to make purely decorative items, while each of the older style of handicrafts was intended to serve a useful purpose.

Carib baskets are quite distinct from other West Indian straw work which is mainly produced from grass or palm leaves. Carib work is produced from the outer skin of the larouma reed and therefore has a firmer texture. The colours are always black brown and off-white woven into various patterns.

The larouma is a slender reed with long leaves. The stems are cut in the forest and brought down to the coast in bundles to dry. Later, some of these are soaked for a few days in mudholes near the river banks. These take on a fine, shiny, black colour, while the others remain a reddish brown. White strands are obtained from the undersides of these brown ones. In this way the Carib craftsmen have three colours to use.

The best Carib panniers are made waterproof by lining the sides with balizier leaves and covering this with another layer of basketry. Woseau reed is used for making bird cages and such things. It was once used for arrow shafts. Wacine-palmiste from the mountain palm, are cut, dried and split and used for baskets. Kaklin roots are also used in this way. Mibi, liane-pomme, liane-grise, calabouli and corde-caco are all local names for types of vine or liana used in basketry.

The ribs of the latanier leaf are stripped and worked before becoming too dry. The outer skin of the Bamboo is stripped off in strands and used for baskets and fishpots and landing kali nets for fishermen. Nowadays, galvanized wire-mesh is used for fishpots. Within the last ten years attractive model sailing ships have been made with bamboo using 'coconut cloth' fibre for the sails. Bakua or shrewpine is used for making the best hats. Coconut and other palm leaves are used for hats and brooms as well.

Vertiver grass is the most popular for mats, although hats are sometimes made with it as well. Dominica's vertiver mats are still considered the best in the Caribbean. Woodcarving and leathercraft are also being developed and coconut shell work is very popular. Before the introduction of plastic foam our mattresses were made

Carib handicrafts (NDC)

of coconut fibres and our pillows stuffed with plain cotton or silk cotton.

One place where the traditions of Dominica's handicrafts can be traced is at the **Old Mill Cultural Centre** at Canefield. A small Museum includes a display of traditional and pre-Columbian artifacts. Also at the Old Mill you can view paintings and sculpture by local and resident artists. Many are intuitive works depicting island scenes and folklore. Some of the work on display is produced by artists trained at the Edna Manley School of Art in Jamaica, among them Earle Ettienne and Arnold Toulon. Other artists who often exhibit here are Georgie, Darius, Eddie John and Kello Royer.

There are also woodcarvings by students of the **Woodcarving Training School** situated on the Old Mill grounds. These carvings are created with the guidance of Haitian sculptor Louis Desiree who has resided here for many years. **Aquarela Galleries**, situated on King George V Street, Roseau, is a commercial gallery which exhibits works by Dominican and Caribbean artists.

| 19 |
Language, folklore and festivals

Language

Even before colonisation, a mixture of languages had taken place in Dominica. The earlier Arawakan/Lokono-speaking people had been conquered by the Karina-speaking Caribs and for a time the two languages were separated between the men and women until, over the years, the Island-Carib language developed in which the Arawakan/Lokono was stronger. In language, at least, the women triumphed in the end.

Dominicans are still some of the greatest users of Island-Carib words because of the late arrival of the Europeans here. Proper and common nouns such as place names, trees and animals are most common in local Creole. The forest mammal, the Agouti; the lizards: abòlò, anoli (Zandoli) and mabouya; Fish: waiwanao (vivano); the birds: sésé (eg sisi zèb), sisserou, pipiri, cayali are just a few. Acoma, cachibou, caconyai, galba and larouma are some plants. The place names can be seen on the map but it is unfortunate that we do not know the meanings of most of them.

The French missionaries, lumbermen and farmers of tobacco, cotton, coffee and food crops were the first Europeans to come in effective contact with the Caribs. The African slaves whom they brought with them, and those who came later, had their origins in many different parts of West Africa with widely varying languages and dialects. The most effective sign and form of conquest is the conquest of language, then ideas and thought patterns follow. Soon the Africans and Caribs were absorbing the French vocabulary, but not without leaving their mark.

French Creole has become the mother tongue and first language of almost all the present population. Though it is easily understood by the Creoles of Guadeloupe, Martinique, St Lucia, Grenada, Trinidad and Haiti, it is identical to none of them and even within Dominica, it can have its slight variations.

The people of the villages of Wesley and Marigot, whose fore-fathers arrived during the last century from the English-speaking Leeward Islands, particularly Antigua, have a dialect all of their own which we call 'cockoy'. No one has seriously studied those speech patterns, but they generally follow the English Creoles of Jamaica and the Lesser Antilles who have another interesting set of origins and word forms.

Folklore and festivals

It was the British mapmakers who divided Dominica into its ten parishes each bearing the name of a saint. But except for legal documents such as land deeds these names and divisions are not generally used. The patron saints of each village receive far more recognition and it is on their feastdays that most of the main village religious festivals occur. Most of these feastdays originated from the mid-nineteenth century, when the Roman Catholic Church was firmly establishing itself, building churches and allocating priests to the scattered village communities which had developed after emancipation. The Roseau Cathedral and most of our older churches date from that period. This is not to say that the influence of the church was not already very strong, but it was a time when, under

The procession at the Feast of Saint Peter

115

such Bishops as Poirier and Naughten, the church was expanding and adapting itself to the social changes which were in progress.

One of the most widely celebrated religious feasts is **Fete La St Pierre** also called the Feast of St Peter and St Paul. This is celebrated during June and July in all of the fishing villages in Dominica. The celebrations do not all take place on the same day but are scattered over a period of weeks so that it is possible, as some fete-lovers do, to drift from village to village following the Fete La St Pierre from Cashacrou up the West Coast along the North East, down to Castle Bruce and Petite Soufriere and around to Fond St Jean and Grand Bay. All the fishing villages have their own style of celebration but it usually consists of a church service (where a certain amount of fish is brought to the church), a procession to the decorated boats for the blessing and then, despite the priest's advice during Mass, the whole village, and all its visitors go *en fete* for the rest of the day with a spate of rum drinking, house visits and dancing way into the night.

Some villages have their own patron saint's feast as well as St Pierre to celebrate. Among them are:

Soufriere	— Our Lady of Lourdes
Pointe Michel	— La Salette
Newtown	— Fatima
Mahaut/Massacre	— St Ann
St Joseph	— St Gerard
Salisbury	— St Theresa
Grand Bay	— St Isadore
Vieille Case	— St Andre
Laudat	— St Ann
Trafalgar	— St Mary Magdalene
Giraudel	— Our Lady of Perpetual Succour

Dates of observance of patron saints days fluctuate. The official date may not coincide with the date on which festivities are observed so that it is impossible, far in advance, to say which village will be doing what on a certain day.

At Grand Bay, **Fete St Isadore** (patron saint of labourers and farmers) is a harvest festival celebrated in a most colourful way. Lourdes, Fatima and La Salette are noted for the pilgrimages people make from other parts of the island to pray at these shrines dedicated to our Lady and her appearance at Lourdes and La Salette in France, and at Fatima in Portugal.

A carnival band of Lilliputians surrounding a giant model of Gulliver as the Thunderbirds Group performs on the streets of Roseau

Fete Les Tou Saintes or All Saints is observed each 1 November when people visit the graves of their departed friends and relatives to light candles and bring flowers. In the evening, the town and village graveyards become a mass of twinkling yellow lights interspersed with the moving silhouettes of visitors in prayer.

One feast which is less widely observed today is **La St Catherine** on 25 November. This day was observed as the best day for planting, transplanting or pruning trees. It was also a good day for cutting hair.

Apart from Christmas and Easter, the biggest festival of the year is **Carnival**. The actual two Carnival holidays of street jump-up are the Monday and Tuesday before Ash Wednesday, but there are calypso and queen contests, shows and parties for at least two weeks before that. All this stems from a mixture of French Roman Catholic traditions and West African costume, song and dance forms. Although masqued balls and Creole fetes were a feature of the French plantocracy throughout the Antilles, street Carnival really blossomed after Emancipation in 1834.

The other annual islandwide festival is Independence Day. Celebrations start in late October leading up to Independence Day itself on 3 November. Village groups compete with each other in competitions of traditional dance, song, storytelling and musical performances. It is also the time when ladies bring out their prized garb, the *grand robe* and *jupe*, their ornate petticoats, jewelry and madras headties to display the finery of Dominica's national dress. The festivals, the language and the folklore associated with it, all reflect the colourful diversity of the island's people and their history.

The Friday before Independence Day is usually observed as Creole Day. School children, office workers and the public put on the National Costume or variations thereof. This recent introduction is observed mostly in Roseau and the bright flashes of madras cloth, sparkling bangles, bracelets and earrings give the streets of the capital a festive air.

On Creole Day hotels and restaurants advertise local cuisine and community groups use the day for fundraising by offering special Creole lunches and snacks at venues around town. The national radio station broadcasts in Creole for the entire day and in theory everyone should go about their business in Creole, although in practice, after a few jovial Creole salutations, just to make the point, most people lapse into English for more complex business transactions.

The music for these festivities is provided by the traditional 'jing-ping' or 'shack-shack' bands. Each band is usually composed of four instruments: the boom-boom, the tambou, the gwage or shack-shack and the accordion. Sometimes violins and banjos are added for extra effect. The jing-ping accompanies the traditional dances such as quadrille, lancers, polka and flirtations.

| 20 |
Dominican cuisine

Dominica's traditional cuisine, like its history, folklore and language, is a reflection of Creole mixture and adaptation since the eighteenth century. The mixture is French, West African and Carib. The adaptation of ingredients was made from what the land provided and what could be conjured up from the staple plantation rations of two hundred years ago. Up to quite recently, before the onslaught of consumerism in the 1960s, imported foodstuffs were very basic. Salted port (*jel cochon*), codfish (*lamowee*), herring (*hawansaw*), red beans, flour, brown sugar and rock salt were the imports which the cooks had to work with.

By adding fish and game from the sea and forest, fruit and vegetables from the field, with a liberal variety of herbs and spices, miracles were conjured up. Cooks worked over coalpots and smoky open hearths called *potagé* or even on the rural peasant's *twa woche*: three large, round volcanic stones placed so as to support the single family pot. Above the open fireplace was the smoke-rack for preserving fish, meat and game such as manicou and agouti.

Some slave plantation terms for food are still in common use today. When you hear people say 'provisions', they mean specifically the root tubers: dasheen, yam, tannia, sweet potato and cush-cush, which were the staple weekly provisions for estate labour.

There were no written recipes. Ingredients and amounts were relayed from one generation to the next by apprenticeship and example. The prima donnas of Dominican cuisine were the 'grand mulatress' wives of the town merchants and estate owners, and the cooks who commanded their smoky kitchens and whose culinary skills were the toast of the island. Through them, we have inherited many fine examples of Creole cuisine. Perhaps the best recipe book on the subject has been produced by one of the descendants of the grand old Dominican families, Yolande Cools-Lartigue, who compiled *The Art of Caribbean Cooking*, published in Canada by Koolart Press, Richmond, British Columbia.

By reviewing the local ingredients, we can get a taste of the dishes

Limes, plantains, christophenes, pawpaws and pigeon peas – some of the exotic produce available in the Roseau market place (CAROL KANE)

they produce. Not all of what is mentioned here is readily available at most restaurants. Much depends on supply and the hunting season, in the case of crabs, crapaud (mountain chicken), river fish and game. We must remember that it is very different to hunt, forage and fish for small scale local consumption, than it is to satisfy a growing mass market of hotels and restaurants. The environmental balance must be borne in mind, and the restricted hunting season of 1 September to the end of February must be strictly adhered to.

Fruit and vegetables pose no such dilemma. Most meals will begin with *callaloo* soup, made from the very young leaves at the heart of the dasheen plant. Most places serve it finely pureed and flavoured with coconut cream. The more traditional callaloo is filled with crab claws, tannia or yam root tubers and dumplings, called *dombway*.

The root tubers or 'provisions' used in Dominica are tannias, dasheen, and various types of yam. One of the best is the violet tinted cush-cush, which has a lighter consistency than most yams. There is the wild yam of the forest called *wa-wa* and another nut-like tuber called *topi-tambu*. Carib cassava can be boiled as a vegetable, but it is more often served in the form of flour, processed by the traditional methods used before the arrival of Columbus. This gritty *fawine* is eaten with crushed avocado pear known locally as *zaboka*.

Green bananas are boiled and are an important part of every meal. Plantain, which is a species within the banana family, is boiled or cut into slices and fried. *Cockoy* is another member of the family and is prepared in the same manner as the plantain. The ripe banana can be the base for several desserts: flambé, fritters, cake, milk shakes, puddings, etc.

The Breadfruit was brought to the Caribbean by Captain Bligh of Mutiny on the Bounty fame, in 1793. These were off-loaded in St Vincent and we got our original plants from there. It took time for suspicious slaves to adopt this new fruit onto their menu. They christened it *yampen* or 'yam bread', and it eventually became as Caribbean as callaloo. It can be boiled and chopped into segments, mashed, or chopped into salads; pickled; beaten and fried and served as croquettes; or roasted. The great thing to do on picnics is to put a whole breadfruit into the wood fire and leave it until the skin is totally charred. Then you open it up, take out the heart, spread with butter, sprinkle with salt and share. This *yampen woti* is a national favourite.

All of these starches can be used in a dish of West African origin we call *ton-ton*. Green bananas, for instance, are put into a *mach pillon* or wooden mortar and are pounded by a pestle in the African fashion. Plantain, dasheen, breadfruit or mixtures of these can be used. The *ton-ton* is then served with gravy, stew and other vegetables. Talking of stews and callaloo, these are often enriched both in calories and flavour by cooking them with coconut milk. This method is called *sankotch coco*.

Our shellfish category has stuffed crab backs at the top of the list. Made of black land crabs, highly seasoned, a stuffed crab back even comes with its own spoon made of part of the claw. River crayfish, *kwibish* and a smaller, prawn-like species called *bouk*, are boiled and served in Creole sauce; fried in batter or served cold in salads. Conch, called *lambi*, and lobster are popular seafoods. Our lobsters are not like the large-clawed New England variety, but are spiney *langousts* which inhabit the coral reefs, particularly along the north coast. Octopus or *chatu* is another delicacy from this area.

Imported salted fish has, over two hundred years, become an island delicacy of sorts. Seasoned and pounded salt cod, *lamowee* creates the popular *boljow* served with bread. Along with this is the seasoned smoked herring, *hawansaw*. The latter is often served on its own with lots of chopped cucumber, onion and chives.

Fresh fish would require a chapter of its own, with sections on broiling, baking, frying and on the multitude of possible sauces to go with each dish. The most popular fish are flying fish or *volan*, king fish, dolphin fish or *dorado*, tuna or *ton*, cavali, bonito, red fish, jacks, balaou, snapper, grouper and garfish or *zorfi*.

Freshwater river fish are not often served in restaurants, since they are in very limited supply. The minute river fry called *titiri* are seasonally available, usually served as *titiri ackras*, crisply fried in batter. Otherwise, they are boiled and served with rice. A favourite fish dish is the *braff*, or *kou bouyon*, a clear fish stew with green bananas, 'provisions', cabbage and *dombway*.

The crapaud is at the head of our meat list. This large frog has had its true nature disguised by being called a 'mountain chicken'. This, I suppose, was for the benefit of timid visitors who would be alarmed at eating frog. Actually, it does taste very much like chicken, and since the back legs are the only parts used, you can believe that you are munching on little drumsticks. Crapaud legs are either fried or stewed in sauce.

The wild Agouti and Manicou are also available during the hunting season. The meat has a strong, gamey flavour and is best smoked or stewed. The wild pigeons, the *ramier* and *pedrix*, are rarely served in restaurants and are seldom available even in private homes, except in those of hunters.

On weekends and festive days, Dominicans enjoy specialties such as 'goat water', a light stew of goat meat. There is also Black Pudding and Souse. Black pudding is a local, highly seasoned, often peppery blood sausage. Souse is salted pork trotters chopped, seasoned, boiled and served cold in its bouillon. Another delicacy is *fwachin*, made in a similar way from cow's skin.

For dessert, we call on the talents of the descendants of the old French families, who adapted tropical fruit into a splendid buffet of pastries, cakes, sweets and preserves. Here are a few of the temptations in store for the visitor with a sweet tooth: 'Guava cheese', sold commercially by Bello Products as 'Guava Delight'; *Fwais* tarts, using our wild mountain strawberries, which look more like raspberries; Mamee apple jam and ice cream made from our local version of apricot, called *zabwico; paté banane*, using plantain; grated coconut sweets called *tablet* and fudge from coconut cream. There are light, floury *baignes* like round doughnuts. West Indian cherries, high in Vitamin C, make excellent jam, pie filling and fruit

Flying fish in Creole sauce, breadfruit puffs, fruit and vegetables

juice. The traditional Creole *gateau* and the dark rum-drenched fruit cakes can be bought at pastry shops such as 'Fran's' on Great George Street, Roseau.

To accompany your meal, you may wish to try one of the many fresh fruit juices which are served in all hotels and restaurants. Even neighbouring Caribbean visitors comment on the variety available here. You can choose from lime, orange, grapefruit, passionfruit, West Indian cherry, pineapple, guava and tamarind, among others. An interesting beverage is *sea moss*, made from a certain type of seaweed. It is collected along reefs and rocks covered by shallow water. It is dried in the sun and then processed to produce a thick, white drink not unlike a vanilla milk-shake. It earns some of its popularity from its reputation as an aphrodisiac.

| 21 |
Reference section

Basic facts

Air travel

By connecting flights with international airlines through Antigua, St Lucia, Guadeloupe, Martinique, Barbados and Puerto Rico. Dominica has no jet airport, but the Caribbean Airline, **LIAT**, provides several daily scheduled flights for the inter-island hop, both northbound and southbound, enabling connections to be made with the rest of the Caribbean. **Air BVI, Air Guadeloupe** and **Air Martinique** have scheduled flights to Dominica. **Nature Island Express** operates scheduled flights to and from its base at Canefield Airport.

Climate

Daytime temperatures vary between 75 – 90°F, the coolest months being from December to March. It can be much cooler in the mountains. It is usually dry, particularly on the western coast, between the months of January and June. Rainfall varies from 50 inches on the coast to 300 inches in the mountainous areas.

Clothing

Casual. Light summer wear, adding a sweater for evenings up in the mountains. Swimwear may NOT be worn in the streets.

Currency

US$1.00 = EC$2.65, subject to fluctuation.
Banks open: 8.00 am – 1.00 pm Mondays to Thursdays
(Royal Bank of Canada and National Commercial Bank
8.00 am – 2.00 pm)
Fridays: 8.00 am – 1.00 pm, 3.00 pm – 5.00 pm;
(Royal Bank of Canada 8.00 am – 4.00 pm).

Time zone

One hour ahead of Eastern Standard Time. Four hours behind GMT

Electric current

220 – 240 volts, 50 cycles. A transformer is needed for American appliances.

Customs regulations

There are no restrictions placed on the amount of money a person may bring in to the country. The following items are admitted duty free: personal or household effects which have been in use for at least 1 year; 40 ounces of spirits or wine, 200 cigarettes or half-pound of tobacco or 50 cigars, per adult; instruments and tools to be used for the purpose of a person's trade, profession or holiday pursuits.

Documents required

No passports or visas are required from US or Canadian citizens, but proof of citizenship (such as a valid passport, a birth certificate or voter's registration card) and an onward or return ticket are required. Income tax clearance is also required on leaving the island only if business has been conducted. This can be obtained from the Income Tax Office on High Street in Roseau.

Departure tax

EC$15.00 per person.

Vaccination requirements

Not required unless the visitor is arriving from an endemic area.

Marriage regulations

One of the partners must have resided in Dominica for at least 15 days. If a special license is required, the reason why must be given. Completed application form, birth certificate and proof of divorce (if applicable) are required. License costs EC$150.00

Communications

Direct telephone, telegraph, fax and telex services to all parts of the world, operated by Cable & Wireless (West Indies) Ltd. DBS Radio, the National Radio, covers the entire island on medium wave band 14 hours a day, broadcasting in English with some French Patois. Voice of the Islands and Voice of Life are religious radio stations. Marpin TV Cable Service and Video One TV are transmitted.

School children at Petite Soufriere (DR PETER EVANS)

Religious services
Roman Catholic, Methodist, Anglican, Pentecostal, Baptist, Church of Christ, Seventh Day Adventist, Jehovah's Witness, Baha'i and various other denominations.

Water
Clean, swift-flowing streams provide our water source, and catchment reservoirs are well maintained. Water is drinkable from the taps or in the high mountain streams. Bottled spring water is also available.

Excursions to neighbouring islands
By sea: Caribbean Express operates a daily fast ferry service to and from Guadeloupe, Martinique and St Lucia. Agents are HHV Whitchurch & Co on Old Street. A limited amount of rough passenger accommodation is available weekly through local shipping agents and boat charters to neighbouring islands are available at some hotels.
By air: LIAT, Air Guadeloupe, Air Martinique, Air BVI and Nature Island Express offer daily flights to neighbouring islands.

Transportation
Public transportation is available and there is a private minibus and

truck service between the capital and the rest of the island, mainly to facilitate movement of school-goers, workers and shoppers. It is advisable to check rates and timing with drivers before boarding. Bus stops at: Valley Road near Police Headquarters for buses to Trafalgar and Roseau Valley; Old Market (for south) and West Bridge (west and northbound), Queen Mary Street (eastbound). Taxis are available. Taxi, bus and minibus drivers communicate in English and local French Patois. Taxis (4 to 6 passengers), minibuses (15 passengers), Land Rover and Ford Jeeps (8 to 10 passengers). Taxis charge by the person when coming from the airports.

Visitors' driving permits may be obtained upon presentation of a valid driver's license to the Police Traffic Department at Roseau, Portsmouth and the airports, for a fee of EC$30. Driving is on the left side of the road.

Vehicle rentals

Anslem's Taxi Service & Car Rental
3 Great Marlborough St.
Roseau,
Commonwealth of Dominica
Tel: 809-44-82730

Budget Rent-a-Car
Canefield Industrial Estate
Canefield
Commonwealth of Dominica
Tel: 809-44-92080
Fax: 809-44-81111

CNC Rent-a-Car
PO Box 310
Roseau,
Commonwealth of Dominica
Tel: 809-44-82207/96375

DEA's Bike Rental
21 Winston Lane, Goodwill,
Commonwealth of Dominica
Tel: 809-44-85075

STL Rent-a-Car
PO Box 21, Goodwill Road
Commonwealth of Dominica
Tel: 809-44-82340/84525
Telex: 8664 Spritad Do

Valley Rent-a-Car
PO Box 3
Roseau,
Commonwealth of Dominica
Tel: 809-44-83233
Telex: 8615 Valsales

Wide Range Car Rentals
81 Bath Road
Roseau
Commonwealth of Dominica
Tel: 809-44-82198
Cable: TI KAI

Shillingford Car Rental
10 Winston Lane, Goodwill
Commonwealth of Dominica
Tel: 809-44-83151

Travel agencies

Da Costa and Musson Travel Agency, Old Street, Roseau. Tel: (809) 448 – 2250.
LIAT Travel Agency, Victoria Street, Roseau. Tel: (809) 448 – 2421/2423.
Whitchurch Travel Agency, Old Street, Roseau. Tel: (809) 448 – 2181.

Tour holidays

The best natural history tour holiday on Dominica is the specialised
Travellers Tree Tour, a comprehensive two week package limited to not
more than 14 persons at a time. Contact Travellers Tree Tours, 116
Crawford Street, London W1H 1AG. Tel: 071 935 2291 or 071 720 5983.
Local tour operators offer both planned and personalised island-wide tours.
For further information contact:

Antours
PO Box 428
Roseau
Commonwealth of Dominica
Tel: 809 – 44 – 86460
Manager: Anison Rabess

Kens Hinterland Adventure Tours
PO Box 447
Roseau
Commonwealth of Dominica
Tel: 809 – 44 – 84850
Tel: 809 – 44 – 83517 (after hours)
Manager: Ken George Dill

**Dominica Tours and Anchorage
Waitukubuli Dive Centre**
PO Box 34
Roseau
Commonwealth of Dominica
Tel: 809 44 – 82638
Telex: 8619
Fax: 809-44-85860
Manager: Mrs Janice Armour

Dive Dominica Limited
PO Box 363
Roseau
Commonwealth of Dominica
Tel: 809 – 44 – 82188
Fax: 809-44-86088

Cable: CASCOM
Manager: Derek Perryman

Emerald Safari Tours
PO Box 277
Roseau
Commonwealth of Dominica
Tel: 809 – 44 – 84545
Telex: 8625 Telagy Do
Manager: Peter Kaufmann

La Robe Creole Tours and Travel
PO Box 270
Roseau
Commonwealth of Dominica
Tel: 809 – 44 – 84436/82896
Telex: 8607 Hotels Do
Fax: 809-44-85212
Manager: Bernadette Francis

Mally's Tour and Taxi Service
Cork Street, Roseau
Commonwealth of Dominica
Tel: 809-44-83114

**Nature Island Taxi & Tour
Service**
PO Box 364, Point Michel
Commonwealth of Dominica
Tel: 809-44-83397/83163

Nature Tours of Dominica
2 Greens Lane
Goodwill
Commonwealth of Dominica
Tel: 809-44-83706

Paradise Tours
4 Steber Street
Pottersville
Roseau
Commonwealth of Dominica
Tel: 809 – 44 – 85999/91648
Fax: 809-44-84134

Rainbow Rover Tours
PO Box 3
Roseau
Commonwealth of Dominica
Tel: 809 – 44 – 88650
Telex: 8625 Telagy Do
Manager: Ivor Rolle

Wilderness Adventure Tours
81 Bath Road
Roseau
Commonwealth of Dominica
Tel: 809 – 44 – 82198
Cable: Ti Kai
Manager: Albert Astaphan

Hospitals

Princess Margaret Hospital – Roseau 82231/8
Portsmouth Hospital – 55237
Marigot Hospital – 57091
Grand Bay Hospital – 63706
All serious cases are sent to Roseau for treatment. Health clinics staffed by district nurses are open every day in the main villages.

Coast guard

A coast guard base at Woodbridge Bay, Roseau, is on call to assist in emergencies within the territorial waters of Dominica. It is a division of the Commonwealth of Dominica Police Service.

Information centres

Tourist Information Booth: The Old Market Plaza. Brochures, maps, hotel and tour guide information.
Tourism Division, NDC: Bath Estate Compound. For more detailed information.
National Parks Office: Forestry Building, Botanic Gardens. Booklets and pamphlets on parks, trails, wildlife, etc., for sale.
Roseau Public Library: Victoria Street next to Fort Young Hotel. Research material on all aspects of the island.

Shopping

Roseau is the centre for all basic supplies: food, medicine, equipment. Portsmouth and some of the larger villages have grocery stores.

There are handicraft shops in Roseau and Portsmouth. Carib craft shops are dotted along the roadside through the Carib Territory.

Entertainment

Some hotels have regular dinner time entertainment one day a week supplied by musicians such as Pembo or Ivor and Helen Rolle. Big dances or shows are occasionally held and feature singers such as Ophelia and Levi Loblack or the Dominican Folk Singers. Daryl Phillip and the National School of Dance or the Waitukubuli Dance Troupe also perform. The main live bands are the Swinging Stars, WCK, Root Stems and Branches, First Serenade and Radication Squad among others.

Discotheques

Action is usually confined to weekends.
Aquacade, – Rockaway Beach, Canefield.
Cannons, – Fort Young Hotel, Roseau.
Saman Tree, – Old Street, Roseau.
Nitebox, – Potters Street, Pottersville.
Wharehouse, – Check Hall, Canefield.

Further information

Contact the following addresses:
The Dominica Hotel Association
PO Box 384
Roseau
Commonwealth of Dominica
Tel: 809-44-86565

Dominica Tourist Division
National Development Corporation
Bath Estate
Roseau
Commonwealth of Dominica
Tel: 809 – 44 – 82186/82351

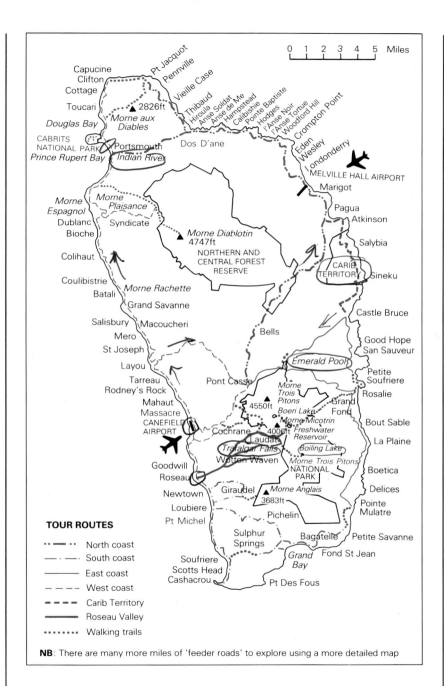

TOUR ROUTES

- ••·•– North coast
- –·–·– South coast
- —— East coast
- – – – West coast
- ▬ ▬ ▬ Carib Territory
- ▬▬▬ Roseau Valley
- •••••• Walking trails

NB: There are many more miles of 'feeder roads' to explore using a more detailed map

Dominica

Where to stay

A thumbnail sketch of our hotels and guest houses follows.

In the mountains

Emerald Bush Hotel: Rustic 'A' frame cabins in the forest a mile from the Emerald Pool and Trois Pitons National Park. No electicity, no telephone, no television. Streams, birds and flowers. Messages and bookings through Tel: 809-44-85998;

Emerald Pool Hotel: 6 rooms in estate house next to Emerald Bush Bar and Hotel. Contact through Tel: 809-44-85998.

Layou River Hotel: Beach resort architecture situated in a river valley. Excellent river bathing. 48 rooms.

Layou Valley Inn: Isolated hilltop eyrie overlooking Layou Valley, with views across to Trois Pitons National Park. 7 rooms.

Papillote Wilderness Retreat: Just before Trafalgar Falls, within lush rain forest gardens. Natural hot mineral pools. 7 rooms.

Springfield Guest House: converted old plantation house with period furniture. Set in a deep, green valley four miles above Canefield, along the Imperial Road. 7 rooms.

On the beach

Castaways Beach Hotel: At Mero on the west coast. Own tennis court. Short drive to Layou River and is on the road to Portsmouth. 27 rooms.

Coconut Beach: 6 rooms and 5 cottages on Picard Beach, Prince Rupert's Bay. Beach bar and restaurant. Popular with neighbouring medical students.

Picard Beach Cottages: Self-contained units on Picard beach with Flambeau Bar and Restaurant and yacht jetty on premises.

Portsmouth Beach Hotel: Just along the beach from Coconut Beach. Own swimming pool. Beach bar. 76 rooms also used by students from nearby medical school.

Purple Turtle: Two very simple rooms with the sand at your doorstep. Bar and restaurant attached. On the beach near Cabrits National Park.

Sunshine Village: Basic bungalows on reclaimed cove at foot of the Cabrit hills. Umbrella restaurant and beach bar. German cuisine. 6 rooms.

On the seafront

Anchorage Hotel: One mile south of Roseau. Own pool, squash court, scuba, watersports and tour facilities. 36 rooms.

Castle Comfort Guest House: Pleasant guest house next to Anchorage. Centre for 'Dive Dominica' scuba tours. 10 rooms.

Evergreen Hotel: Family link with Castle Comfort next door. Set in small botanic garden. Noted for fine island food and service. 7 rooms.

Indian River Inn: On the Portsmouth waterfront near to the Indian River. Basic guest house facilities with bar looking across the harbour.

Sisserou Hotel: Just along the road from Castle Comfort and Evergreen hotels. Swimming pool. 20 rooms.

Roseau and environs

Hotels

Excelsior Hotel: In suburban Canefield next to the airport. 12 rooms. Conference room.

Fort Young Hotel: Set within the 18th century fort which once guarded the town. All 33 rooms look over the ramparts to the sea. Courtyard pool, bar and conference centre.

Goodwill Inn and Restaurant: 3 rooms on Federation Drive within easy walk of central Roseau. Tel: 809-44-85998.

Reigate Hall Hotel: 17 rooms on a hillside overlooking Roseau and surrounding valleys. Tennis court and pool.

Guest houses

Case Ropa: Portsmouth main street. Basic self-contained rooms with snack bar on premises.

Cherry Lodge: Old West Indian flavour at 20 Kennedy Avenue. Bar attached. 8 rooms.

Continental Inn: 37 Queen Mary Street. Bar. 10 rooms.

Kent Anthony: Great Marlborough Street. Bar. 21 rooms.

Vena's: Cork Street. The birthplace and childhood home of novelist Jean Rhys. 14 rooms. Linked to tree-shaded courtyard restaurant: The World of Food. Vena also offers 4 rooms in the countryside along the Transinsular Road near Pont Cassé.

Laudat

Roxy's: Basic six room guest house in mountain village within easy reach of all the main sights of Trois Pitons National Park. Guides live on the premises and are available for Boiling Lake and other guided hikes. Bar.

Marigot

Thomas Guest House: 3 basic rooms in the centre of Marigot Village on the north-east coast.

Carib Territory

Olives Guest House: Rooms in a traditional West Indian house, set in a colourful garden. At Atkinson on the border with the Carib Territory.
Charles Williams Guest House: Near Salybia. Run by a Carib couple who will also guide you around the Carib Territory.
Floral Gardens: On the banks of the Pagua River at Concorde near the western border of the Carib Territory, this guest-house is set in a colourful garden near river pools.

North coast house rentals

Hampstead House: Large estate house overlooking coconut groves within walking distance of beach and river pools. Contact: Douglas, Portsmouth. Tel: 809-44-55253

Pointe Baptiste: Two houses overlooking sandy coves near Calibishie. Set in 20 acres of private woodland. Five minute walk down to the beaches. Contact: Mrs Geraldine Edwards, Calibishie. Tel: 809-44-57322

Red Rocks Haven: Three cottages overlooking Petite Baptiste Bay, Calibishie. Five minute walk to beach. Contact: Mrs Rose Aird. Tel: 809-44-82931

Where to eat

The main hotels welcome outside diners, preferably with reservations a couple of hours in advance. Roseau restaurants mainly cater for the lunchtime crowd, but are open throughout the day. The pick of Roseau is:

La Guiyave on Cork Street. Set in a charming old Roseau town house with shady verandah tables overlooking the street below. Cheerful, usually busy atmosphere. Good local dishes, directed by cook-owner Hermina Astaphan.

The Orchard on King George V Street. Situated in a spacious mid-town bungalow with traditional portico entrance and tiled courtyard. Fine local cuisine under direction of cook-owner Joan Cools-Lartigue.

La Robe Creole, probably Dominica's most renowned restaurant. Situated on Victoria Street, just down the road from Fort Young and the Cenotaph. Excellent menu served by staff in traditional island dress. Cook and partner Tony and Erica Burnette-Biscombe.

La Robe Creole Restaurant

World of Food, in its shady courtyard setting, beneath a spreading mango tree on Queen Mary Street, is a popular meeting place for lunches and dinners.

Snack bars and simpler restaurants are all over town. Among them are **The Green Parrot** and **The Cartwheel** on the Bayfront, **Hope, Creole Kitchen, Kwees, Raffoul's Snackette** and **Mange La Place** at the Old Market, **Trends, Saman Tree** and the **Pina Colada Bar**.

Those at Portsmouth are: **Five Star** on Harbour Lane and **Purple Turtle** at the north end of Lagon. **The Cabin, Bound-to-Groove, Casa Ropa** and **Indian River Inn** on Bay Street and **Prince Rupert's Tavern** at the Cabrits.

At Calibishie: **Almond Tree Beach Bar and Restaurant**.

On Donkey Beach at Canefield the **Shipwreck** specialises in seafood.

The **Bush Bar** is set in rain forest garden overlooking streams just one mile beyond the Emerald Pool on the Castle Bruce Road.

135

What to read

History

The Dominica Story by Lennox Honychurch (available in Dominica). Only up-to-date history (to 1984) of the island, interwoven with information on Dominica's geography, natural history, folklore, the arts and social customs. Illustrated with photographs and Lennox Honychurch's own drawings. Comprehensive and readable.

Caribbean Landmarks also by Lennox Honychurch (Nelson) tells the cultural and racial history of the region through its historic sites and events. General, but a helpful background.

Our Island Culture by Lennox Honychurch. Folk traditions of Dominica (published locally).

Travel

The Traveller's Tree by Patrick Leigh Fermor (Penguin Travel Library). Beautifully written, with an insightful chapter on Dominica. First published in 1950.

Touch the Happy Isles by Quentin Crewe (Michael Joseph, hardback; Headlines, paperback). Recent travelogue. Includes enthusiastic chapter on Dominica.

Caribbean Style (Thames & Hudson). Glossy, coffee-table book with wonderful pictures of Caribbean interiors and gardens – both grand and not so grand. Disappointing text. Concentrates on the French islands but the influences cross the cultural divide.

The following include sections on Dominica:

Frommer's Dollarwise Guide to the Caribbean
Cadogan Guides – The Caribbean by Frank Bellamy;
Fodor's Guide to the Caribbean.

Natural History

Birds of the West Indies by James Bond (Collins). Classic identification guide, first published in 1936 and now in its fifth edition. Colour and black and white illustrations. Useful to all, from experts downwards.

Birds of the Eastern Caribbean by Peter Evans (Macmillan).

Collins Guide to Tropical Plants by Wilhelm Lotschert and Gerhard Beese. Descriptions, colour photographs and useful background information on tropical vegetation. For professionals and amateurs.

Caribbean Wild Plants and their Uses by Penelope N Honychurch (Macmillan). Illustrated with drawings by the author, an expert on native flora of the tropics. Describes plants, their folklore and how they are – or were – used as remedies for illness.

Trees of the Caribbean by S A Seddon and G W Lennox (Macmillan). Basic guide to the more common trees for those with little botanical knowledge – with good colour photographs.

Flowers of the Caribbean by G W Lennox and S A Seddon (Macmillan). Companion to the above book and with a similar format.

Butterflies and Other Insects of the Eastern Caribbean by P D Stilling (Macmillan). Another simple guide with good, clear colour photographs.

Native Orchids of the Eastern Caribbean by Professor Julian Kenny (Macmillan). Basic guide, lots of colour photographs.

Fiction

The Orchid House by Phyllis Shand Allfrey (Virago). The author was a white Dominican – writer, poet and politician. First published in 1953 and reissued in 1982. Nostalgic novel of three white sisters returning to their tropical island birthplace. Evokes the sensuousness of Dominica, which Allfrey so loved.

Tales of the Wide Caribbean by Jean Rhys (Heinemann). Collection of short stories that draw on Rhys' Dominican background and reveal the lasting impression that it made on her 'exile' in Europe.

Wide Sargasso Sea by Jean Rhys (Penguin). Her most famous novel, part of which – vividly and hauntingly – is set in Dominica.

Other Rhys fiction – *Tigers Are Better Looking, Sleep It Off Lady* and *After Leaving Mr Mackenzie* (all Penguin) also contain resonances of her Dominican childhood. *Smile Please* (Andre Deutsch), snatches of her uncompleted autobiography. Much is about Dominica, which she left as a teenager, only once to return.

Out of print (both non-fiction) but worth looking out for:

The Sugar Islands by Alec Waugh (Cassell, 1958).

The Baths of Absalom by James Pope-Hennessy (Allan Wingate, 1954).

MACMILLAN CARIBBEAN GUIDES SERIES
Titles available

Antigua and Barbuda: The Heart of the Caribbean – Dyde
The Bahamas: A Family of Islands – Saunders
Barbados: The Visitor's Guide – Hoyos
The Islands of Bermuda: Another World – Raine
Belize: Ecotourism in Action – Cutlack
Cuba: Official Guide – Gravette
Curaçao Close-Up – Heiligers-Halabi
Dominica: Isle of Adventure – Honychurch
Grenada: Isle of Spice – Sinclair
Islands to the Windward: Five Gems of the Caribbean
   (St Maarten/St Martin, St Barts, St Eustatius, Saba, Anguilla) – Dyde
Jamaica: Fairest Isle: An Introduction and Guide – Sherlock
   and Preston
Montserrat: Emerald Isle of the Caribbean – Fergus
Nevis: Queen of the Caribees – Gordon
St Kitts: Cradle of the Caribbean – Dyde
St Lucia: Helen of the West Indies – Ellis
St Vincent and the Grenadines – Sutty
Trinidad and Tobago: A Guide and Introduction – Taylor
The Turks and Caicos Islands: Lands of Discovery – Smithers
The British Virgin Islands: Treasure Islands of the
   Caribbean – Shepard